This Textbook is useful for Savitribai Phule Pune University and other Universities of Maharashtra as well as Competitive Exams.

History

Art and Architecture in Early India

(HIS - 509 MJ)

M.A. - I (Sem. - I)

As per New Education Policy (2020)

Prof. Prashant Pawar
(B.Sc., LL.B., M.A. (AIH & C)., M.A. (History).,
LL.M.(Buss.Law), M.Phil., SET)
MVP Samaj's Arts, Commerce and Science College,
Tryambakeshwar, Nashik.

2023

AF529334

Price - 95/ -

SUCCESS PUBLICATIONS

Published by
Dr. Rajesh M. Patne
Success Publications
Radha Krishna Apartment, 535, Shaniwar Peth,
Appa Balwant Chowk, Opp. Prabhat Talkies, Pune - 411 030.
Ph. 24434662, Mobile : 9325315464.

Edition
2023

Edited By
Mr. Valmik Gaikwad

Typesetting, Layout
Mr. Valmik Gaikwad

Cover Designing
Miss. Varsha Lokhande

ISBN NO. – 978-81-19180-84-4

Preface

It is a matter of great pleasure for us to present this book to our esteemed readers. This book has been designed as standard text on 'Art and Architecture in Early India' for M. A. (History) (Sem. - I).

This book comprehensively covers the entire syllabus of M.A. (History) Course of Savitribai Phule Pune University effective from 2023 onwards. It has been written to meet the requirements of students of M. A. (History). Some of the special features of the book are as follows:

1. *Full coverage of the revised syllabus of M. A. (History).*
2. *Chapter outline at the beginning of each chapter to give a bird's eye view of the topics covered in the chapter.*
3. *Point wise explanation of each topic in the chapter.*
4. *Topics are logically arranged in numbered paragraphs exactly according to the modified syllabus.*
5. *Proposed questions at the end of each chapter.*
6. *Extensive use of diagrams, tables and various forms to give visual view of key concepts and techniques.*
7. *Conversational, lucid and simple language.*

Every effort has been made to provide the readers with most up-to-date and authentic material on the subject.

We are very grateful to our publisher Mrs. and Mr. Rajesh Patne who have rendered all possible assistance in bringing out this book. We wish to acknowledge our deep gratitude to staff who have assisted and helped us in preparing this book. We will consider our efforts amply rewarded in case the book proves useful to the students and teachers of the subject.

Suggestions of readers are welcome and shall be acknowledged with gratitude.

With best wishes.

By Authors

Syllabus

M. A. - I (Sem. - I) History

Art and Architecture in Early India (HIS-509 MJ)

Unit	Topic	Lecture
1	**Introduction to Indian Art and Architecture**	**08**
	a. Prehistory b. Harappan Civilization c. Mauryan Period	
2	**Buddhist and Jain Architecture**	**10**
	a. Stupa Architecture – Sanchi, Bharhut, Amravati, Sarnath b. Monasteries and Chaityas c. Paintings in Buddhist and Jain Art	
3	**Sculptures, Paintings and Rock - Cut Architecture in India**	**12**
	a. Bhimbetaka b. Bagh, Ajanta, Ellora and Tanjore c. Symbolism of Temple Architecture d. Gandhara style, Mathura Style, Naagar Style, Dravid Style	

INDEX

M. A. - I (Sem. - I) History

Art and Architecture in Early India (HIS-509 MJ)

UNIT 1

Introduction to Indian Art and Architecture

Introduction:

Indian art and architecture is a rich and diverse tapestry that spans millennia, reflecting the country's profound cultural, religious, and historical evolution. From the intricate rock-cut temples of Ellora and Ajanta, showcasing the fusion of Buddhist, Hindu, and Jain influences, to the awe-inspiring elegance of Mughal monuments like the Taj Mahal; Indian architecture showcases a seamless blend of innovation and tradition. The vibrant sculptures and frescoes of ancient sites like Khajuraho depict both earthly and divine narratives with exceptional craftsmanship, while the intricate patterns of Mughal miniature paintings evoke a sense of refined beauty. Indian art is characterized by its spiritual underpinnings, evident in the elaborate iconography of Hindu deities and the serene Buddha sculptures of Sarnath. Diversity is a hallmark, with regional variations such as the colorful Madhubani paintings of Bihar and the intricate Pattachitra art of Odisha. These artistic expressions mirror India's multicultural society, where architecture and art become vessels for preserving and transmitting cultural identity, mythologies, and philosophical wisdom through generations.

1.1 Prehistory:

Pre-history, in the context of the division of history, refers to the period of human history before the invention of writing systems and the emergence of recorded historical accounts. It is a time when humans relied on oral traditions, cave paintings, artifacts, and archaeological evidence to understand and reconstruct the past. Pre-history, the division of history before the invention of writing is typically divided into three major periods: the Paleolithic Era, the Mesolithic Era, and the Neolithic Era. Indian art and architecture during prehistory encompass a vast and intriguing span of time, offering glimpses into the early creative expressions of the Indian subcontinent.

1.1.1 Paleolithic Era:

The Paleolithic era, often referred to as the Old Stone Age, spans a vast period of human history, beginning around 2.6 million years ago and ending around 10,000 BCE. It was characterized by the emergence of early Homo species and their gradual evolution into anatomically modern humans. During this extended epoch, humans engaged in nomadic lifestyles, subsisting primarily through hunting and gathering. The art and architecture of the Paleolithic era offer intriguing insights into the cognitive, cultural, and creative capacities of these ancient humans. In following discussion we will delve into the art and architecture of the Paleolithic era, exploring their significance, characteristics, and the enduring legacy they leave behind.

A) Art of the Paleolithic Era:

The art of the Paleolithic era is a testament to the cognitive development and creative expression of early humans. This art manifests in the form of cave paintings, portable art, and symbolic artifacts.

1) Cave Paintings and Rock Art:

One of the most iconic features of Paleolithic art is the cave paintings found in various locations around the world, such as Lascaux in France and Altamira in Spain. These paintings were created using a variety of techniques, including pigments derived from natural sources like minerals and charcoal. The subjects of these paintings often included animals that were central to the Paleolithic people's survival, such as bison, deer, horses, and mammoths. These images, rendered with a surprising level of realism and attention to detail, suggest both an appreciation for the natural world and a desire to document it. Some paintings also include human figures, often in stylized and symbolic forms.

2) Portable Art:

In addition to cave paintings, Paleolithic humans also created portable art in the form of small figurines, beads, and other artifacts. These objects were typically crafted from materials like bone, ivory, stone, and clay. The most famous example of portable Paleolithic art is the "Venus figurines." These small sculptures depict exaggerated female forms with emphasized breasts, hips, and buttocks. The precise meaning of these figurines is still debated among scholars, with interpretations ranging from fertility symbols to representations of idealized beauty.

3) Symbolism and Engravings:

Paleolithic humans also engaged in symbolic expression through engravings and carvings on stone surfaces. These abstract markings, often found on tools and personal ornaments, suggest an emerging capacity for abstract thought and the use of symbols to communicate or convey meaning.

B) Architecture of the Paleolithic Era:

While the Paleolithic era is not typically associated with permanent architectural structures due to the nomadic lifestyles of early humans, there are instances of architectural features that provide insights into their living spaces and technological innovations.

1) Shelters and Dwellings:

Early Paleolithic humans likely lived in temporary shelters made from readily available materials such as animal hides, sticks, and leaves. These structures were simple and portable, enabling them to move as they followed food sources. Over time, some groups may have developed more sophisticated forms of shelters, such as huts made from wooden frames covered with animal skins. While there is limited archaeological evidence of such structures, the knowledge required to build and modify shelters demonstrates a level of architectural awareness.

2) Fire Use and Hearths:

The controlled use of fire marked a significant technological advancement during the Paleolithic era. Early humans used fire not only for warmth and protection but also for cooking food and altering the properties of materials. The presence of hearths and fire pits in archaeological sites reflects their understanding of fire's importance.

C) Significance and Legacy:

The art and architecture of the Paleolithic era hold profound significance in understanding the development of human cognition, culture, and creativity.

1) Cognitive Evolution:

The ability of early humans to create art and use symbols suggests the emergence of cognitive faculties such as abstract thinking, imagination, and the capacity to communicate ideas beyond immediate needs.

2) Cultural Expression:

Paleolithic art represents the earliest form of cultural expression, reflecting the beliefs, values, and experiences of these ancient humans. The representations of animals and humans in art could have held ritualistic, symbolic, or communicative meanings.

3) Technological Advances:

The use of pigments, carving tools, and the mastery of fire showcased the Paleolithic people's innovative use of available resources, paving the way for future technological developments.

4) Continuity:

The themes and motifs found in Paleolithic art can be seen as precursors to artistic traditions that would emerge in later periods, continuing to influence artistic expressions throughout history.

D) Challenges and Interpretations:

Interpreting Paleolithic art and architecture comes with its own set of challenges due to the lack of written records and the temporal gap separating modern researchers from these ancient creators.

1) Symbolic Meanings:

Deciphering the symbolic meanings of Paleolithic art is a complex endeavor, as these societies lacked written records to explain the intentions behind their creations. Various interpretations, ranging from spiritual significance to social communication, have been proposed by scholars.

2) Cave Context:

Understanding the purpose of cave paintings and the environments in which they were created requires careful analysis of archaeological contexts. Researchers must consider factors such as lighting, accessibility, and potential ritualistic activities within the caves.

3) Survival Bias:

The preservation of Paleolithic art and architecture is influenced by geological and environmental factors. Many artistic creations might have been lost to the passage of time, making it difficult to fully grasp the diversity of artistic practices during this era.

1.1.2 Mesolithic Age:

The Mesolithic Age, often referred to as the Middle Stone Age, is a significant transitional period in human prehistory that spans roughly from 10,000 BCE to 6,000 BCE. This era follows the Paleolithic Age and precedes the Neolithic Age. During the Mesolithic Age, humans experienced significant environmental changes, technological advancements, and shifts in lifestyle that had a profound impact on their artistic expressions and architectural practices. In following discussion, we will explore the art and architecture of the Mesolithic Age, examining their characteristics, cultural significance, and contributions to human history.

A) Art of the Mesolithic Age:

The art of the Mesolithic Age marks a continuation and evolution of the creative traditions established during the Paleolithic era. However, it also reveals new innovations driven by changing environmental conditions and the emergence of more settled lifestyles.

1) Portable Art and Personal Adornments:

Mesolithic humans continued the tradition of creating portable art in the form of small sculptures, figurines, and personal ornaments. These objects were often crafted from materials such as bone, antler, ivory, and stone. The smaller scale of these artifacts suggests that they might have held personal or ritualistic significance.

Some Mesolithic figurines depict animals and humans in a more naturalistic style than their Paleolithic counterparts. This suggests a growing understanding of anatomy and an increased focus on representation.

2) Rock Art and Petroglyphs:

Rock art and petroglyphs were prevalent during the Mesolithic Age, providing insights into the social and cultural aspects of these ancient societies. While cave paintings were still created, open-air rock surfaces also became canvases for artistic expression. Petroglyphs often featured a variety of subjects, including animals, humans, geometric patterns, and abstract symbols. These engravings might have held ritualistic or communicative purposes, and their presence across different regions suggests a shared visual language.

B) Architecture of the Mesolithic Age:

The architectural practices of the Mesolithic Age were influenced by changing environmental conditions, innovations in tool making, and shifts in subsistence strategies. While permanent structures were still relatively uncommon, temporary shelters and communal spaces began to exhibit new features.

1) Semi-Permanent Shelters:

Mesolithic humans continued to construct temporary shelters, but these structures often featured more sophisticated construction techniques. For example, dwellings might have been built using a combination of wooden frames and animal hides, creating more durable and weather-resistant structures.

2) Hunting and Gathering Camps:

The semi-settled lifestyle of Mesolithic communities led to the establishment of more structured hunting and gathering camps. These camps featured arrangements of huts or tents, communal fire pits, and evidence of tool production and resource processing.

3) Communal Spaces:

As human societies became more settled, communal spaces for gatherings and rituals likely began to emerge. These spaces might have been marked by features such as hearths, central fire pits, and arrangements of stones or natural features.

C) Cultural Significance and Contributions:

The art and architecture of the Mesolithic Age offer insights into the evolving cultural, social, and cognitive developments of early humans.

1) Cultural Continuity and Change:

The art forms and architectural practices of the Mesolithic Age reflect both continuity from the Paleolithic era and the emergence of new artistic conventions. This dynamic period laid the foundation for future artistic expressions.

2) Environmental Adaptation:

Changes in environmental conditions, such as the transition from glacial to interglacial periods, influenced Mesolithic societies' artistic and architectural choices. The semi-permanent shelters and resource management strategies demonstrated a growing ability to adapt to changing landscapes.

3) Social Interaction and Rituals:

The emergence of communal spaces and the presence of petroglyphs suggest a heightened emphasis on social interaction and rituals. These spaces could have played a role in fostering group cohesion, sharing knowledge, and engaging in symbolic practices.

4) Technological Advances:

Mesolithic humans continued to innovate in tool making, leading to advancements in crafting techniques and the creation of more intricate portable art objects.

D) Challenges and Interpretations:

Interpreting the art and architecture of the Mesolithic Age presents challenges similar to those faced when studying earlier periods of prehistory.

1) Cultural Context:

The lack of written records makes it challenging to fully understand the cultural and symbolic meanings behind Mesolithic art and architecture. Researchers must rely on archaeological context, comparative studies, and ethnographic observations.

2) Chronological Variability:

The Mesolithic Age spans a significant timeframe and varies across regions. Artistic and architectural practices might differ based on local environmental conditions, resource availability, and cultural interactions.

3) Preservation Issues:

Many artifacts and architectural remains from the Mesolithic Age have been lost to natural degradation, erosion, and human activity. This loss limits our understanding of the full extent of artistic expressions during this era.

1.1.3 Neolithic Age:

The Neolithic Age, often referred to as the New Stone Age, is a transformative period in human history that marked a significant shift from hunting and gathering to agriculture and settled life. This era spans from around 10,000 BCE to 2,000 BCE, and it witnessed the emergence of agricultural practices, domestication of animals, and the establishment of permanent settlements. The Neolithic revolution not only transformed human subsistence strategies but also had a profound impact on art and architecture. In following discussion we will explore the art and architecture of the Neolithic Age, examining their characteristics, cultural significance, and contributions to human civilization.

A) Art of the Neolithic Age:

The art of the Neolithic Age reflects the changing lifestyles and cultural shifts brought about by the adoption of agriculture and the establishment of settled communities. Neolithic art is characterized by its focus on themes related to agriculture, fertility, and communal life.

1) Ceramics and Pottery:

One of the most significant artistic developments of the Neolithic Age was the widespread production of ceramics and pottery. The shift from nomadic to settled life necessitated vessels for food storage, cooking, and domestic use. Neolithic pottery exhibits a variety of shapes, sizes, and decorations. Many pottery items were adorned with intricate designs, geometric patterns, and sometimes even representations of animals and human figures. The use of pottery not only served practical purposes but also enabled artistic expression and creativity.

2) Megalithic Monuments and Structures:

Neolithic communities engaged in monumental construction projects, creating large-scale stone structures that have left an enduring legacy. One of the most iconic examples of Neolithic architecture is the megalithic monument, characterized by the use of massive stones for construction.

a) Dolmens:

Dolmens are composed of large, flat stones placed horizontally on upright stone pillars to create a chamber or portal-like structure. These structures are often associated with burials and might have held ritualistic or commemorative significance.

b) Cromlechs:

Cromlechs, commonly known as stone circles, are circular arrangements of standing stones. These structures are thought to have served as ceremonial spaces or markers of astronomical events.

c) Menhirs:

Menhirs are single, vertically placed stones that can vary in size from small to monumental. They might have been used as markers, symbols of religious or social significance, or even as memorials.

3) Figurines and Statuettes:

Neolithic communities continued the tradition of creating figurines and statuettes, often representing human figures and animals. These artifacts are thought to have had ritualistic or symbolic meanings related to fertility, agriculture, and the spiritual beliefs of these communities.

B) Architecture of the Neolithic Age:

The architectural achievements of the Neolithic Age reflect the transition from temporary structures to more permanent settlements. The advent of agriculture led to the establishment of villages and towns, necessitating innovative architectural approaches.

1) Domestic Architecture:

Neolithic settlements were characterized by circular or rectangular huts made from a combination of materials such as wood, thatch, and clay. These dwellings often featured wattle and daub construction, where a framework of wooden stakes was covered with mud and clay. The use of permanent materials like clay and wood marked a departure from the temporary shelters of earlier periods. The construction of these structures demonstrated a more settled and organized way of life.

2) Communal and Ceremonial Structures:

In addition to domestic architecture, Neolithic communities constructed communal and ceremonial structures. These might include large buildings for communal gatherings, ritualistic practices, and perhaps even early religious ceremonies. Neolithic longhouses are examples of such communal structures. These elongated buildings often had a central hearth and were used for various purposes, including living quarters, workshops, and communal activities.

C) Cultural Significance and Contributions:

The art and architecture of the Neolithic Age hold profound cultural significance and offer valuable insights into the evolving social and economic dynamics of early human communities.

1) Agricultural Revolution:

The adoption of agriculture during the Neolithic Age brought about significant changes in human lifestyles. This shift is reflected in the artistic representations of fertility, crops, and domesticated animals.

2) Settled Communities:

The transition from nomadic to settled life led to the establishment of permanent villages and towns. Neolithic architecture, such as domestic huts and communal structures, reflects the social cohesion and organization of these communities.

3) Ceremonial Practices:

The construction of megalithic monuments and the creation of figurines suggest that Neolithic communities engaged in ritualistic practices related to fertility, death, and spirituality. These practices likely played a role in solidifying group identities and maintaining cultural traditions.

4) Technological Advancements:

The development of pottery and the construction of megalithic structures required innovative technological solutions. These achievements demonstrate the Neolithic people's mastery of materials and construction techniques.

D) Challenges and Interpretations:

Interpreting Neolithic art and architecture poses challenges due to the scarcity of written records and the temporal gap separating modern researchers from these ancient societies.

1) Cultural Context:

The symbolic meanings behind Neolithic art and architecture are often speculative, as the absence of written records makes it challenging to fully understand the cultural significance of these creations. Interpretations are based on archaeological context, comparative studies, and ethnographic observations.

2) Variability:

Neolithic art and architecture exhibit significant regional variability. Different cultures and communities adopted unique artistic styles and architectural practices, making it important to consider local contexts when analyzing artifacts and structures.

3) Preservation Issues:

The preservation of Neolithic artifacts and architectural remains is influenced by natural degradation, erosion, and human activities. Many ancient structures and objects have been lost over time, limiting our understanding of the full extent of Neolithic artistic expressions.

1.1.4 Chalcolithic Age:

The Chalcolithic Age, also known as the Copper Age or Eneolithic Age, represents a critical phase in human history characterized by the transition between the Neolithic and Bronze Age. This period witnessed significant advancements in metallurgy, the development of early urban centers, and the emergence of more complex societies. The art and architecture of the Chalcolithic Age reflect the evolving cultural, technological, and social dynamics of ancient communities. In following we will explore the art and architecture of the Chalcolithic Age, examining their characteristics, cultural significance, and contributions to human civilization.

A) Art of the Chalcolithic Age:

The art of the Chalcolithic Age showcases a continuation of artistic traditions from earlier periods, but with notable advancements driven by innovations in metallurgy and the establishment of more complex societies.

1) Metalwork and Metallurgy:

One of the defining features of the Chalcolithic Age is the use of copper and other metals in artistic production. The mastery of metallurgy allowed ancient communities to create tools, ornaments, and decorative items with increased durability and aesthetic appeal. Copper objects from this period include tools, weapons, jewellery, and votive offerings. The increased availability of metal tools likely facilitated the production of more intricate and detailed art forms.

2) Terracotta Figurines:

Terracotta figurines continued to be a prominent form of artistic expression during the Chalcolithic Age. These figurines depict humans, animals, and deities, reflecting both religious and societal themes. The figurines often feature realistic details, capturing the clothing, hairstyles, and facial features of the period. This suggests a heightened awareness of human anatomy and an interest in representing these aspects in art.

3) Ceramics and Pottery:

Ceramics remained a significant artistic medium during the Chalcolithic Age. Pottery vessels were used for utilitarian purposes as well as for artistic expression. Chalcolithic pottery is characterized by intricate designs, geometric patterns, and motifs that reflect the cultural and social dynamics of the time. The development of firing techniques allowed for the creation of more durable and aesthetically pleasing ceramics.

B) Architecture of the Chalcolithic Age:

The Chalcolithic Age saw the continued evolution of architectural practices, driven by technological advancements, changing settlement patterns, and the emergence of more complex societies.

1) Settlements and Urban Centers:

During the Chalcolithic Age, some communities transitioned from small villages to larger settlements with more complex layouts. These settlements often featured urban planning, specialized structures, and communal spaces. Early urban centers, such as Mehrgarh in the Indus Valley and Çatalhöyük in Anatolia, provide insights into the architectural innovations of the period. Çatalhöyük, for instance, had tightly packed houses with roofs that served as walkways, demonstrating a unique architectural approach to space utilization.

2) Stone Architecture:

While stone had been used for architectural purposes in previous periods, the Chalcolithic Age witnessed advancements in stone construction techniques. Stone structures became more prominent in urban centers and larger settlements.

3) Tholos Tombs:

Tholos tombs are distinctive stone burial structures with beehive-shaped roofs. These tombs showcase the Chalcolithic people's architectural skills and cultural practices related to burial and commemoration.

C) Cultural Significance and Contributions:

The art and architecture of the Chalcolithic Age offer insights into the changing social, technological, and cultural dynamics of ancient societies.

1) **Metallurgical Innovation:**
The development of metallurgy and the use of copper and other metals in artistic production marked a significant technological advancement. This innovation not only improved the durability of tools and objects but also enabled the creation of more sophisticated art forms.

2) **Emergence of Urban Centers:**
The transition from villages to urban centers reflects increasing social complexity and the development of more organized and specialized societies. Urban planning and specialized structures laid the foundation for future urban civilizations.

3) **Symbolism and Rituals:**
The presence of terracotta figurines, pottery, and stone structures suggests the continuation of ritualistic and symbolic practices. These artifacts might have held religious, social, or cultural significance for the Chalcolithic communities.

4) **Interactions and Trade:**
The spread of metal objects, pottery styles, and architectural influences suggests interactions and trade networks between different Chalcolithic communities. These interactions played a role in the exchange of ideas and cultural practices.

D) **Challenges and Interpretations:**
Interpreting Chalcolithic art and architecture presents challenges due to the scarcity of written records and the temporal gap separating modern researchers from these ancient societies.

1) **Cultural Context:**
The symbolic meanings behind Chalcolithic art and architecture often require speculation, as the absence of written records makes it challenging to fully understand the cultural significance of these creations. Interpretations rely on archaeological context, comparative studies, and ethnographic observations.

2) **Regional Variability:**
Chalcolithic art and architecture exhibit significant regional variability, influenced by local environments, resources, and cultural interactions. Different communities adopted unique artistic styles and architectural practices, making it important to consider local contexts when analyzing artifacts and structures.

3) **Preservation Issues:**
The preservation of Chalcolithic artifacts and architectural remains is influenced by natural degradation, erosion, and human activities. Many ancient structures and objects have been lost over time, limiting our understanding of the full extent of Chalcolithic artistic expressions.

1.2 Harappan Civilization:

The Harappan Civilization, also known as the Indus Valley Civilization, is one of the most intriguing and enigmatic ancient cultures that thrived in the Indus River valley and parts of western India and Pakistan during the Bronze Age. Spanning from approximately 3300 BCE to 1300 BCE, this advanced urban civilization left behind an extensive archaeological record that provides valuable insights into their art, architecture, society, and way of life. In following discussion we will delve into the art and architecture of the Harappan Civilization, exploring their characteristics, cultural significance, and enduring legacy.

A) Urban Planning and Architecture:

The Harappan Civilization was a highly developed urban culture that emerged in the floodplains of the Indus River and its tributaries. It is characterized by its sophisticated urban planning, advanced drainage systems, and a script that remains undeciphered to this day. The civilization is named after Harappa, one of the major archaeological sites where its remains were first discovered.

1) Mohenjo-Daro:

It was situated in the Larkana province of Sindh. It was spread in around one square mile area. For planning ease, it was divided in to two parts; East and West. Western part is relatively smaller than Eastern one. This space has been elevated by making a platform. Platform has been made by mud mortar and raw bricks. Construction has been done on this platform only. There is fortified wall all around it. This wall is made of raw bricks. There are towers and minarets also in it. There must be a main entrance in this fort, but scholars have not able to know about this. There are several public buildings in this west part. We get to know about prosperity of this place. It appears that different building had different names like; 'Purohitawas', 'Anna Bhandar', 'Mahavidyalaya' etc., but this can only be an estimate, as still there is no success in reading their script. Looking at grandiose of such buildings, it can be said that there must live high profile people. Remains of such a building are found in Mohenjodaro which is standing on bamboos. It is assumed that this was a public hall of the town, where people used to assemble and do meetings. Logic by scholars is that this must be used to have a big market. There were lanes in between houses of Mohenjodaro in its western part. There is information of roads, which can be used to move from one place to other. Many remains of small houses have been found in excavation which indicates that there used to live smaller sections of society. A big pond has been found in this western part of Mohenjo-Daro. It is 39 feet long and 23 feet wide. Use of bricks has been done to make this pond. Bitumen plaster has been done after layering of bricks, so that water cannot go out. This large pond has been described as formal bathing place. Eastern part of Mohenjodaro is relatively larger than western part. Similar to western part, this part also is surrounded by walls. Entire town of western part was based on platform, but not in eastern part. Here houses were made on separate platforms. Platforms perhaps were used for security point of view. Due to platform was higher than eastern part, eastern part was low height. Hence eastern part was called Lower Hillock. There were many houses in this part. Here we have found 3 feet wide roads.

Due to these roads, many houses of eastern part were divided in many groups. Interesting thing is that houses were made up of modern bricks, unlike eastern part, where they used raw bricks. Some houses of eastern parts were double storied also. There was provision to flush out dirty water from it. This dirty water used to come to drainage outside the house. These big drainages were at both sides of big roads. These were made of bricks. Much such drainage was covered from top. Drainages found of Indus period are still an example for us. We get to know by the remains found that there were holes in the drainage which were close to big roads. After they were filled with dirty water, it was flushed out. Archaeological remains clearly tell us that, house cleanliness was a major focus area. There were many wells for the use of common men, which were made of bricks. There used to be one main door in houses of eastern part of Mohenjodaro. These doors used to open the nearing roads. Like modern times, there used to a courtyard in those houses in the middle. There used to be rooms around this courtyard. Sign of door has been found as remains which indicate that each room had one door. There used to be windows also. These windows were at high spots in the walls unlike modern day windows. Such windows can still be seen in the villages of Bihar, which are quite high from ground. To conclude, we can say that houses of Mohenjodaro are not attractive but the methods used to construct them, tells us about the high level efficiency and effectiveness of their style.

2) Harappa:

This place was situated at the left of Ravi River in modern Pakistan. Similar to Mohenjodaro, Harappa too was divided in to two parts on planning point of view. First part was at the eastern side and second at the western side. Unfortunately, practice of stealing bricks by modern people, has actually spoiled the eastern part. Hence, we could not get sufficient remains of this part. As regards, western part, this was surrounded by walls. This part also was based on high platform; it is difficult to tell about fortification of this place, since inner wall bricks have been stolen by modern day people. No such thing has been found in excavation, which could give us some information. Fortification of this western part tells us that, there were many doors for entry and exit. There was one main gate, which opened towards north. Just in front to its north gate, Ravi used to flow. Excavation in between Ravi River and north gate tells us that there was a grain storage house and houses for labourers. Round platforms made of brick also were there. There were small sockets in the platform for keeping grains. The place where common people lived, we have found a graveyard also in south.

3) Chanhudro:

There have been no major excavation in this area; hence many mysteries are still under cover. Remains pertaining to making of many articles have been found. Excavation tells us that there was a bead making unit also.

4) Kalibangan:

This also had two parts. Western part was called western hillock, this part also had fortification but was divided in two parts. Both these fort units were linked. One could go from one fort area from another. Proof of two fortifications in one part reveals that there were separate demarcations for high and rich people. Use of second part was for high level platforms. Remains of Havankund also have been found. To the south of residential area of Harappa, but to the west of Kalibanga, proof of graveyard is found. There are some such remains in the eastern part of this place, which suggest practice of worship and puja etc. Above description is for the western hillock of Kalibanga, information on eastern hillock is also there. A wall is found as remains, which gives us some information about its planning. Its planning is very much similar to Mohenjodaro. Still, there are some differences. Houses of Kalibanga have used raw bricks whereas Mohenjodaro has used modern bricks. There was no provision of flushing out dirty water alike Mohenjodaro. There was shortage of water drainage system. Hence we can say that position of Kalibanga was inferior as compared to Mohenjodaro.

5) Lothal:

An important settlement of Indus civilization was Lothal. It was situated in modern Gujarat. Remains here tell that there were no two hillocks like Kalibanga and other areas, means it was not divided in two parts. It appears that this was a port of Harappa civilization. As per map, this was 360 meter long and 210 meter wide, spread in north- south direction. This too was surrounded by a huge wall. Such boundary was probably done for safety purpose. South-eastern part of the town is like a big platform, which is approximately 4 meter of height. There are many lanes of smaller platforms over it containing many narrow paths. We can recall grain storage house of Mohenjodaro after seeing this huge platform. This platform is of 48.5 x 42.5 meter. There are many buildings at the back of this part of the town and are connected with one drain only. In other part of the town, there were many shops and houses. Major out of them were; factory for bead for necklace, jewelers and tinkers. Main road of this town is from north to south. But a very wonderful achievement is a huge tank made up of bricks measuring 219 x 27 meters and its height is 4.5 meters. This is to the east of Lothal town and next to grain storage house. There must be a door at one point of this tank to control flow of water, just like used in modern Dams. It appears that it was port of Lothal, but this view is not accepted in general. Objective of making this tank is still not clear. Some scholars consider it small micro port, but scholars have rejected this logic as well.

6) Surkotda:

Here we have found only one hillock. Alike, Kalibanga this too was surrounded by walls. There were two separate boundaries connected with each other. It appears that here too, in one part rich used to live and other part was meant for worship. The part of religious rituals had higher platform. There was a graveyard in its western side. Thus, we see the replica of Kalibanga' western hillock planning here. There is no eastern hillock.

7) Banwali:

This place had planning similar to Surkotda and Kalibanga. Here also there were two boundaries connected with each other. In one part, rich used to live and other was used for worship.

8) House Construction:

Above mentioned town planning tells us that, Indus people not only lived in big small, mud and brick work houses, but also paid attention to the cleanliness of houses also. Bricks used for house construction were red, baked and strong. Bricks were heated in fire with wood fire. Excavation reveals small brick size as; 10.25 inches long and 5 inches wide. Another smaller brick has been found of 5 inches long and 2.25 inches wide. There is also one big size brick. This is 20.25 inches long, 10 inches wide and 3.5 inches thick. Archaeological analysis reveals that buildings of Indus civilization were made as per planning. Houses remains tell us that normally houses were 30 feet long and 26-27 feet wide. Rich people had double or at times treble the sizes of these normal houses. We have found remains of double or treble storey houses as well in Indus civilization. Walls were quite thick from security point of view, remains of plastering rooms and wooden plastering have also been found. For the planned development, importance of drainage construction for water disposal is important. In Indus valley also we get to know about drainage. They used to be wooden and bricks stairs to go to first floor within houses. Width of such stair was around 1.25 feet. Due to threat of flood, houses were normally made on high platforms. There used to be hearth of clay and bricks for making food similar to modern times. There were separate kitchens, where huge pots were fixed in the ground. Houses had many rooms. These rooms had doors of around 3.75 feet width. There used to be big doors also in some big houses. Doors were of normally of one side only, so that apart from humans, cattles or vehicles could also walk past it. Normally, each house had square bathrooms. Its floor used to be very smooth. It was made of modern bricks. Bathrooms had water provision for bathing. Water used to be kept in big pot. Toilet used to be near bathroom. Water from bathroom used to go to toilet through small drains. This water kept toilets clean. Toilet water used to merge into road side drainage. There used to be a small drain between toilet and bathroom. Similarly, there was a small drain between toilet and drainage. To stop water from skidding away, side bricks were used to be smooth by rubbing so their joints used to stick together. Looking at planned housing, water arrangement, cleanliness etc., it can be assumed that there must be some public body for taking care of town management. Indus civilization gives us information about our ancient town life and civilization.

9) Town Planning:

The excavations of the ruins at Harappa showed a remarkable skill in town planning and organisation. The city was divided into the smaller citadel area covering the western part and the larger residential area to the east. The essential institutions of civic life and places for public rituals were generally located in the citadel area which had defence walls and bastions along with elaborate entrances. Probably, the citadel area was the locus of wealth and hence it had to be demarcated from the common area. In social and economic terms, this demarcation shows that the society was divided into rich and poor classes. The main streets and roads were set in a line, sometimes running straight for a mile and varying in width from four meters to 10 meters. Most of these roads and streets were paved with fire burnt bricks. On either side of the street, stood houses of various sizes, but not any of them protruding into the streets. The main streets intersected at right angles dividing the city into squares or rectangular blocks each of which was subdivided, lengthwise and crosswise into lanes. Some buildings had lamp posts and also wells. There was an elaborate drainage system which emptied into the river.

10) The Drainage System:

The drainage system of the Harappan Civilisation was very advanced. The drains were covered with slabs. Water flowed from houses into the street drains, which had manholes at regular intervals. People were expected to use pits in which heavier parts of the rubbish would settle down, while only sewerage water was allowed to drain off. All such pits and drains were occasionally cleaned by workmen. In every house, there were a well-constructed sink and water allowed from the sink into the underground sewers in the streets. This elaborates drainage system shows that the people of Harappa were fully conversant with the principles of health and sanitation.

B) Art and Artifacts:

Art and artifacts in harappan civilization explain with following points:

1) Seals and Script:

The Harappan people are known for their intricately carved seals made of materials like steatite. These seals feature depictions of animals, humans, and composite creatures. Some seals also contain an as-yet-undeciphered script, highlighting their advanced communication and administrative systems.

2) **Terracotta Figurines:**

Terracotta figurines have been found at various Harappan sites. These figurines depict human and animal forms, often showcasing a high degree of craftsmanship and detailing. They provide insights into clothing, hairstyles daily life during that era.

3) **Ceramics:**

Harappan pottery includes a variety of forms such as storage jars, bowls, and perforated vessels. The pottery is often well-made and exhibits intricate designs, including geometric patterns and animal motifs.

4) **Metalwork:**

While less common than other materials, metal artifacts have been found, including objects made of copper, bronze, and gold. These objects range from tools and ornaments to sculptures, showcasing the Harappans' skill in metallurgy.

C) **Cultural Significance and Legacy:**

Explain with following points:

1) **Advanced Urbanization:**

The planned cities, advanced drainage systems, and multi-storied structures of the Harappan Civilization highlight their sophistication in urban planning and architecture.

2) **Trade and Connectivity:**

The presence of seals with animal motifs and script suggests a well-organized trade network. The civilization likely had connections with regions as far away as Mesopotamia.

3) **Religious Practices:**

The presence of the Great Bath and evidence of fire altars at various sites indicate that the Harappans had religious rituals and practices. The seals and figurines might also have had religious or symbolic significance.

4) **Social Organization:**

The planned cities and uniformity in construction materials suggest a degree of centralized planning and administration. The script on seals hints at an organized administrative system.

5) **Artistic Aesthetics:**

The art of the Harappan Civilization exhibits a certain aesthetic sensibility, often focusing on natural motifs, geometric patterns, and a high level of craftsmanship.

D) **Challenges and Unanswered Questions:**

Explain with following points:

1) **Undeciphered Script:**

One of the most significant challenges is the inability to decipher the Harappan script. The lack of a readable script limits our understanding of their written language and communication systems.

2) Cultural Decline:

The reasons for the decline and eventual disappearance of the Harappan Civilization remain debated among scholars. Environmental factors, shifts in trade routes, and cultural changes have all been proposed as possible explanations.

3) Religious Practices:

While some structures like the Great Bath suggest possible religious practices, the exact nature of Harappan religious beliefs and rituals is still not fully understood.

1.3 Mauryan Period:

The Mauryan period was a crucial era in Indian history, spanning from around 322 BCE to 185 BCE. It marked the rise of the Mauryan dynasty, which was founded by Chandragupta Maurya and later, expanded and consolidated by his grandson Ashoka the Great. This period witnessed significant developments in various aspects of society, including art and architecture. The Mauryan rulers' patronage of art and architecture played a pivotal role in shaping the cultural landscape of ancient India. In following discussion we will delve into the art and architecture of the Mauryan period, exploring its characteristics, influences, and contributions to Indian heritage.

A) Art during the Mauryan Period:

The art of the Mauryan period was deeply rooted in the prevailing socio-cultural milieu, which was characterized by the amalgamation of diverse influences from different regions of India. The art of this era primarily manifested in sculpture, and to a lesser extent in other art forms like pottery and coinage.

1) Sculpture:

Mauryan sculpture primarily revolved around the representation of religious and secular themes. It displayed a unique blend of realism and symbolism. The hallmark of Mauryan sculpture was the attention to detail, anatomical precision, and a sense of solemnity.

a) Pillars and Capitals:

One of the most remarkable achievements of Mauryan art was the erection of monumental pillars. These pillars were made of polished sandstone and stood as a testament to the architectural prowess of the period. The famous Ashoka Pillars, such as the Sarnath Pillar and the Sanchi Pillar, are prime examples. These pillars were crowned with beautifully sculpted animal capitals, often depicting lions or other animals. The Lion Capital of Ashoka, with its four majestic lions, has become an iconic symbol of India.

b) Yakshas and Yakshis:

Another notable aspect of Mauryan sculpture was the depiction of yakshas and yakshis, which were semi-divine beings associated with fertility and protection. These sculptures showcased a perfect balance between realism and stylization, portraying the human form with a sense of vitality and grace.

c) Stupas:

Stupas, hemispherical structures used for meditation and relic worship, were a central feature of Buddhist architecture during this period. The Great Stupa at Sanchi is a prime example. Its torana (ornamental gateway) and the narrative friezes adorned with scenes from the life of Buddha and Jataka tales are remarkable instances of early Indian narrative art.

2) Pottery and Coinage:

Mauryan pottery was utilitarian in nature, with a focus on functionality rather than elaborate decoration. However, some pottery items did feature intricate designs and patterns. Additionally, Mauryan coins are important artifacts that provide insights into the art and culture of the period. The coins bore inscriptions in Brahmi script and often depicted animal motifs.

B) Architecture during the Mauryan Period:

The architecture of the Mauryan period was characterized by its utilitarian approach, blending elements of both indigenous Indian architecture and the influences of the time. While the architectural remains from this era are limited, they offer valuable insights into the construction techniques and design principles of the time.

1) Palaces and Fortifications:

Chandragupta Maurya's capital city, Pataliputra (modern-day Patna), featured some of the earliest examples of Mauryan architecture. The palace and fortifications were built using wooden structures, which were common during that era. Unfortunately, due to the perishable nature of wood, these structures have not survived.

2) Stupas:

Stupas were central to Mauryan architecture due to their religious significance. The Great Stupa at Sanchi, commissioned by Ashoka, is a testament to the architectural achievements of the era. The stupa was constructed using a simple plan, consisting of a circular base and a hemispherical dome. The torana (gateway) with its elaborately carved pillars and narrative friezes added a decorative aspect to the otherwise plain structure.

3) Pillars and Gateways:

As mentioned earlier, the Mauryan pillars are exceptional examples of architectural and sculptural achievements. These pillars were erected throughout the Mauryan Empire, and many of them were inscribed with Ashoka's edicts. The pillars were often placed at important sites to mark significant events and convey Ashoka's messages of moral and ethical behavior.

C) Influences on Mauryan Art and Architecture:

The art and architecture of the Mauryan period were shaped by a multitude of influences, including indigenous Indian traditions, Achaemenid Persian elements, and Hellenistic styles that were introduced through interactions with Alexander the Great's successors in the northwest of India.

1) Indigenous Indian Traditions:

Mauryan art and architecture drew heavily from indigenous Indian artistic sensibilities. The depiction of yakshas, yakshis, and religious themes resonated with existing beliefs and practices in the Indian subcontinent.

2) Persian Influences:

The Achaemenid Persian influence is visible in some architectural aspects, such as the use of polished stone pillars. This influence might have been a result of the interactions between Chandragupta Maurya and the Achaemenid Empire during his early career.

3) Hellenistic Influence:

The interactions with Hellenistic cultures, particularly those of the Seleucid Empire in Central Asia, also left an imprint on Mauryan art. This is most evident in the depiction of realistic human forms and the use of architectural elements like pillars and capitals.

D) Contributions and Legacy:

The Mauryan period's contributions to Indian art and architecture are enduring and significant. They laid the foundation for subsequent artistic developments in the subcontinent.

1) Architectural Techniques:

The construction of monumental pillars and stupas showcased advanced architectural techniques and engineering skills, setting a precedent for future architectural endeavors.

2) Symbolism and Spirituality:

The Mauryan art's emphasis on symbolism and spiritual themes paved the way for the evolution of religious art in India, particularly in the realms of Buddhism and Jainism.

3) Narrative Art:

The narrative friezes on stupas and gateways at sites like Sanchi introduced the concept of visual storytelling in Indian art, a tradition that continued to flourish in later periods.

4) Inscriptions and Edicts:

The inscriptions on Ashoka's pillars and other structures provided valuable insights into the social, political, and moral concerns of the time, contributing to our understanding of ancient Indian society.

♦♦♦

Review Questions

Q.1. Answer the Following Questions:

1) Explain the Art and Architecture in Paleolithic Era.

2) Write about the Art and Architecture in Mesolithic Age.

3) Explain the Art and Architecture in Chalcolithic Age.

4) Discuss about the Art and Architecture Neolithic Era.

5) Explain the Art and Architecture in Harappan Civilization.

6) Discuss about the Art and Architecture in Mauryan Period.

Q.3. Write Short Notes on:

1) Paleolithic Era.

2) Neolithic Era.

3) Mesolithic Age.

4) Art in Harappan Civilization.

5) Architecture in Harappan Civilization.

6) Mohenjo-Daro.

7) Art in Mauryan Period.

8) Architecture in Mauryan Period.

♦♦♦

UNIT 2

Buddhist and Jain Architecture

Introduction:

Buddhist and Jain architecture, two profound expressions of ancient Indian spiritual and artistic creativity, bear witness to the distinctive ideologies and cultural influences that shaped their construction. Buddhist architecture, characterized by its enigmatic stupas, serene viharas, and ornate chaityas, reflects the core teachings of the Buddha and his path to enlightenment. From the grandeur of the Great Stupa at Sanchi to the remarkable rock-cut caves of Ajanta and Ellora, Buddhist structures offer a fusion of symbolism, simplicity, and reverence. On the other hand, Jain architecture, exemplified by its intricately carved temples and monastic complexes, embodies the principles of non-violence, compassion, and asceticism. The Dilwara Temples of Mount Abu and the stunning Ranakpur Temple stand as exceptional examples of Jain architectural marvels, showcasing the intricacy of marble sculptures and the aspiration for spiritual purity. While Buddhist architecture emphasizes universal truths and enlightenment, Jain architecture celebrates the spiritual journey and liberation from worldly attachments, both contributing to the rich tapestry of India's architectural heritage and inspiring generations with their enduring spiritual resonance and artistic ingenuity.

2.1 Stupa Architecture:

Stupa architecture, a pinnacle of spiritual and artistic expression, encompasses a diverse array of structures across Buddhist cultures, from the majestic hemispherical domes of ancient India, such as the Great Stupa at Sanchi and the Sarnath Stupa, which enshrine relics and symbolize the Buddha's teachings and enlightenment, to the ornate multi-tiered pagodas of East Asia, like the iconic Borobudur in Indonesia and the revered Shwedagon Pagoda in Myanmar, which merge Buddhist principles with local architectural styles. These stupas, whether simple or elaborate, share common elements - a circular base representing the universe, a harmika symbolizing the abode of deities, and an umbrella or chatra denoting spiritual ascent. Stupas also integrate intricate carvings, reliefs, and sculptures that narrate the Buddha's life, Jataka tales, and philosophical concepts, fostering a visual journey through Buddhist teachings. Stupa architecture's transcendence extends to modern times, as innovative interpretations like the Global Vipassana Pagoda in India or the Great Stupa of Universal Compassion in Australia fuse tradition with contemporary materials, reflecting the enduring allure of stupas as vehicles of reverence, meditation, and enlightenment across cultures and eras.

2.1.1 Sanchi Stupa:

The Sanchi Stupa stands as an enduring testament to the profound cultural and spiritual significance of Buddhism in India. Nestled on a hilltop in the state of Madhya Pradesh, India, Sanchi is a site of immense historical and artistic value. The stupa complex, along with its intricate carvings, sculptures, and stupas, provides a window into the rich tapestry of Buddhist art, architecture, and philosophy. Sanchi's history dates back to the 3rd century BCE, during the time of Emperor Ashoka, a prominent figure who converted to Buddhism after the Kalinga War. As a devoted follower of the Buddha's teachings, Ashoka commissioned the construction of numerous stupas across his empire to enshrine relics and promote the spread of Buddhism. Sanchi emerged as one of the most prominent sites for Buddhist worship and pilgrimage during this era.

A) Architectural Features:

The Sanchi Stupa complex boasts an array of architectural features that highlight the craftsmanship of ancient Indian artisans:

1) Hemispherical Dome:

The central architectural element of the stupa is its hemispherical dome, which symbolizes the concept of enlightenment and represents the stupa as the cosmic axis. The dome is a solid structure made of stone and contains relics of the Buddha or other revered individuals.

2) Harmika:

A top the dome, there is a square railing known as the harmika. It represents the abode of the gods and signifies the center of the universe. In early stupas like Sanchi, the harmika is a simple structure, but in later periods, it evolved into more elaborate designs.

3) Chatras (Umbrellas):

The harmika is often crowned with multiple chatras, which are symbolic parasol-like structures. These chatras denote rank and protection and are commonly associated with Buddhism and its teachings.

4) **Toranas (Gateways):**
The Sanchi Stupa is known for its intricately carved toranas or gateways. These gateways are positioned at cardinal points and serve as entrances to the stupa's enclosed space. The toranas are decorated with elaborate relief sculptures depicting scenes from the life of the Buddha, Jataka tales (stories of Buddha's previous lives), and other Buddhist themes.

5) **Relief Sculptures:**
The toranas and other parts of the stupa are adorned with finely carved relief sculptures. These sculptures are not only artistic but also serve didactic purposes, conveying Buddhist teachings and narratives visually to the illiterate masses.

B) Symbolism and Iconography:
Sanchi's carvings and sculptures are replete with symbolism and iconography that communicate Buddhist teachings and philosophy:

1) **Lotus:**
The lotus is a central symbol in Buddhism, representing purity, enlightenment, and the potential for spiritual growth. Many sculptures and carvings at Sanchi feature lotus motifs, underscoring the idea of transcending suffering and achieving enlightenment.

2) **Dharmachakra (Wheel of Dharma):**
The Dharmachakra is a prominent symbol representing the Buddha's teachings. It consists of eight spokes, symbolizing the Noble Eightfold Path. Depictions of the wheel on the toranas and other structures emphasize the importance of following the path to liberation.

3) **Bodhi Tree:**
The Bodhi tree, under which the Buddha attained enlightenment, is often represented through stylized trees in Sanchi's carvings. This symbolizes the transformative experience of awakening and the potential for all beings to achieve enlightenment.

4) **Stupa as Cosmic Axis:**
The stupa's design and upward-reaching form symbolize the axis mundi, connecting the physical and spiritual realms. It represents the center of the universe, linking earth and heaven.

5) **Three Jewels (Triratna):**
The Triratna, comprising the Buddha, Dharma (teachings), and Sangha (spiritual community), is a central concept in Buddhism. This triad is often depicted in Sanchi's art, emphasizing the refuge Buddhists take in these pillars of their faith.

C) Spiritual Significance:
Sanchi remains a pilgrimage destination for Buddhists and a place of reflection for seekers of spiritual wisdom:

1) **Enlightenment and Nirvana:**

The central dome of the stupa represents the concept of enlightenment and nirvana, which are the ultimate goals of Buddhist practice. The dome's shape symbolizes the abode of enlightenment, the highest state of spiritual awakening.

2) **Axis Mundi:**

The Sanchi Stupa is often seen as a representation of the cosmic axis or axis mundi, connecting the earthly realm with the spiritual realm. It serves as a link between different levels of existence, signifying the interconnectedness of all beings.

3) **Circumambulation:**

The practice of circumambulation, or walking clockwise around the stupa, is a form of devotion and meditation. It symbolizes the path to enlightenment and helps practitioners focus their minds on Buddhist teachings while engaging in physical activity.

4) **Relics and Devotion:**

Stupas, including the Sanchi Stupa, often enshrine relics of the Buddha or enlightened beings. These relics are objects of veneration and devotion for Buddhists. The act of making offerings and paying respects to the stupa is a way to cultivate virtues and accumulate positive karma.

5) **Toranas and Teachings:**

The intricately carved toranas (gateways) of the Sanchi Stupa are adorned with relief sculptures that depict scenes from the life of the Buddha, Jataka tales, and other Buddhist narratives. These sculptures serve as visual representations of Buddhist teachings, making them accessible to both literate and illiterate audiences.

D) **Legacy and Influence:**

Sanchi's influence extends beyond its historical context, impacting various aspects:

1) **Art and Architecture:**

The Sanchi Stupa's architectural style and iconographic elements have influenced subsequent Buddhist art and architecture across Asia, leaving an indelible mark on the aesthetics of temples, stupas, and monasteries.

2) **Buddhist Philosophy:**

Sanchi's carvings and reliefs serve as visual aids for understanding Buddhist concepts. The site's art continues to illuminate the Buddha's teachings for both practitioners and enthusiasts.

2.1.2 Bharhut Stupa:

The Bharhut Stupa stands as a remarkable relic from ancient India, a testament to the rich cultural heritage and spiritual legacy of the region. Nestled in the heart of Madhya

Pradesh, this ancient Buddhist site offers a glimpse into the artistic mastery, intricate narratives, and spiritual significance that defined the era. The Bharhut Stupa is more than an architectural monument; it's a window into the evolution of art, philosophy, and devotion during the early phase of Buddhism. The origins of the Bharhut Stupa date back to the 2nd century BCE, during the Mauryan period. At this time, Buddhism was flourishing, and Emperor Ashoka played a pivotal role in spreading its teachings. The stupa was an integral part of this expansion, serving as a site of veneration, pilgrimage, and artistic expression.

A) Architectural Features:

The Bharhut Stupa complex is characterized by its architectural features, which offer insights into the artistic and cultural sensibilities of the time:

1) Stupa Structure:

The Bharhut Stupa follows a traditional stupa design, consisting of a hemispherical dome (anda) on top of a raised platform or drum (harmika). The dome represents the cosmic universe, while the harmika symbolizes the sacred axis connecting the earthly and celestial realms.

2) Gateway (Torana):

One of the distinctive features of the Bharhut Stupa is its elaborately carved toranas or gateways. These toranas are placed at the cardinal points of the stupa and are adorned with intricate relief sculptures depicting various scenes from the life of the Buddha, Jataka stories (stories of the Buddha's previous lives), and other Buddhist themes.

3) Relief Sculptures:

The stupa is renowned for its sculptural artistry. The reliefs on the toranas and other parts of the stupa portray stories and events related to the life of the Buddha, important Buddhist symbols, and scenes of daily life from ancient India. The sculptures provide valuable insights into the clothing, hairstyles, jewelry, and material culture of that period.

4) Yakshis and Yakshas:

Apart from Buddhist narratives, the reliefs also include depictions of yakshis (female nature spirits) and yakshas (male counterparts) that were part of pre-Buddhist and local religious beliefs. These figures add a local touch to the otherwise Buddhist-themed artwork.

5) Lotus Motif:

The lotus motif is prominently featured in the architectural elements and sculptural decorations of the Bharhut Stupa. The lotus, a symbol of purity and enlightenment in Buddhism, is often seen in the carvings, adorning the railings and gateways.

B) Symbolism and Iconography:

The Bharhut Stupa is a significant archaeological site in India that showcases remarkable symbolism and iconography within its structure and ornamentation. It is an ancient stupa, a type of Buddhist monument, located in the modern-day state of Madhya Pradesh. The stupa dates back to the Mauryan period (circa 2nd century BCE) and provides valuable insights into the artistic and religious expressions of that time. Let's explore the symbolism and iconography of the Bharhut Stupa:

1) Yakshi Figures:

One of the most iconic features of the Bharhut Stupa is the presence of Yakshi figures. These female figures are depicted as tree goddesses, often shown sensuously entwined with the branches of flowering trees. The Yakshis symbolize fertility, abundance, and the life-giving force of nature. Their presence highlights the reverence for the natural world and its cycles.

2) Jataka Stories:

The Bharhut Stupa is adorned with numerous reliefs depicting Jataka stories—tales of the Buddha's past lives before attaining enlightenment. These narratives serve didactic purposes, conveying moral lessons and teachings. The Jataka stories depicted on the stupa's railing illustrate the virtues of compassion, self-sacrifice, and ethical conduct.

3) Pillars and Gateways:

The gateways and pillars of the Bharhut Stupa are elaborately carved with scenes from the Buddha's life, as well as various symbols and motifs. These carvings are a visual representation of the Buddhist doctrine and narrative. They emphasize the life of the Buddha, his teachings, and the path to enlightenment.

4) Chakravartin Wheel:

The depiction of the chakravartin wheel, symbolizing the "Wheel of Law," is another prominent feature. This wheel represents the Buddha's teachings and the cycle of birth, death, and rebirth (samsara). The depiction of the wheel signifies the dissemination of the Dharma the Buddha's teachings across the world.

C) Spiritual Significance:

Here are some aspects of its spiritual significance:

1) Connection to the Buddha:

The Bharhut Stupa is believed to have been constructed during a time when the historical Buddha, Siddhartha Gautama, had recently passed away. The stupa serves as a tribute to the Buddha and his teachings. The scenes depicted on the stupa's reliefs often revolve around the life and teachings of the Buddha, emphasizing his role as the enlightened one who offered a path to liberation.

2) **Representation of the Dharma:**

The carvings and iconography on the Bharhut Stupa vividly depict the Buddha's teachings, known as the Dharma. Scenes from the Jataka stories, ethical parables, and moral lessons are intricately carved into the stupa's surfaces. These visual narratives serve as a reminder of the principles of compassion, wisdom, and ethical conduct that the Buddha imparted to his followers.

3) **Spiritual Journey:**

The Bharhut Stupa's architecture and symbolism reflect the Buddhist understanding of the spiritual journey. The presence of the chakravartin wheels—a symbol of the Buddha's teachings—represents the cyclic nature of existence and the pursuit of enlightenment. The lotus motif, with its growth from the mud to the blossoming flower, symbolizes the transformation of the individual from ignorance to enlightenment.

4) **Meditation and Contemplation:**

Stupas are not just physical structures; they are also considered objects of meditation and contemplation. The stupa's presence and symbolism offer a focal point for Buddhist practitioners to engage in meditation, reflection, and the cultivation of mindfulness. The peaceful environment of the stupa provides a conducive setting for individuals to connect with their inner selves and deepen their spiritual practice.

5) **Sacred Geometry and Cosmic Symbolism:**

The design of the Bharhut Stupa incorporates sacred geometry and cosmic symbolism, reflecting the Buddhist worldview of interconnectedness. The arrangement of elements mirrors the cosmic order, emphasizing the interconnected nature of all life and the unity of the universe. This symbolism reinforces the Buddhist understanding of the interdependence of all phenomena.

D) **Influence and Legacy:**

The Bharhut Stupa's influence extends beyond its historical context, leaving a lasting impact on various aspects:

1) **Artistic Heritage:**

The intricate carvings and reliefs of the Bharhut Stupa have influenced subsequent generations of artists and craftsmen, inspiring their creative endeavors.

2) **Buddhist Philosophy:**

The site's carvings serve as visual aids for understanding Buddhist concepts, making the teachings more accessible and relatable to both practitioners and enthusiasts.

2.1.3 Amravati Stupa:

The Amravati Stupa stands as a remarkable testimony to the flourishing artistic and spiritual legacy of ancient India. Nestled along the banks of the Krishna River in Andhra Pradesh, this monumental stupa complex holds within its intricately carved reliefs and architectural grandeur, the essence of a bygone era when Buddhism thrived and artistic expression flourished. The Amravati Stupa is more than a relic; it's a journey into the artistic mastery, religious devotion, and cultural richness of early Buddhist civilization. The Amravati Stupa was constructed during the Satavahana dynasty's reign, flourishing between the 2nd century BCE and the 2nd century CE. This era marked a pivotal period in Indian history where Buddhism not only gained prominence but also became a vibrant cultural force. The stupa's creation was a manifestation of the widespread acceptance and reverence for the teachings of the Buddha.

A) Architectural Features:

Following are the architectural features of Amravati stupa:

1) **Stupa Structure**:

   The Amravati Stupa follows the traditional stupa design with a central hemispherical dome (anda) atop a raised platform or drum (harmika). The dome represents the cosmos, while the harmika symbolizes the axis connecting the earthly and spiritual realms.

2) **Circular Platforms**:

   The stupa is built on a circular base that consists of multiple platforms or terraces. These platforms create a stepped appearance and serve as a foundation for various decorative elements.

3) **Balustrades and Railings**:

   Elaborate stone railings and balustrades encircle the stupa's circular platforms. These railings are adorned with intricate sculptural carvings depicting various scenes from the life of the Buddha, Jataka stories, and other Buddhist narratives.

4) **Toranas (Gateways)**:

   The Amravati Stupa features several beautifully carved toranas or gateways at the cardinal points of the stupa. These gateways are richly ornamented with relief sculptures that narrate Buddhist stories and teachings.

5) **Relief Sculptures**:

   The sculptural decorations of the Amravati Stupa are a major highlight. The reliefs portray the life of the Buddha, his previous incarnations (Jatakas), stories from Buddhist scriptures, and various celestial beings. These sculptures provide insights into the artistic style, clothing, and social context of the time.

B) Symbolism and Iconography:

The Amravati Stupa's carvings and sculptures are replete with symbolism and iconography that convey Buddhist teachings and principles:

1) **Lotus Symbolism:**
The lotus, representing purity and spiritual growth, appears prominently in carvings. Its depiction signifies the journey from ignorance to enlightenment.

2) **Bodhisattvas and Deities:**
Sculptures of Bodhisattvas and celestial beings communicate compassion, wisdom, and spiritual aspiration. Their presence emphasizes the path towards Buddhahood.

3) **Wheel of Dharma:**
The Wheel of Dharma, symbolizing the Buddha's teachings and the Eightfold Path, is a recurring motif in carvings. Its presence underscores the centrality of these teachings.

C) **Spiritual and Significance:**
The Amravati Stupa holds immense spiritual and significance, transcending time and space:

1) **Relic Enshrinement:**
Like many stupas, the Amravati Stupa was initially constructed to enshrine relics of the Buddha or other revered monks. The presence of these relics symbolizes the physical connection to the Buddha's teachings and his enlightened state.

2) **Teaching Through Art:**
The stupa is adorned with elaborate relief sculptures that depict scenes from the life of Gautama Buddha, stories from his previous lives (Jataka tales), and other significant events from Buddhist narratives. These carvings served as a visual medium for conveying Buddhist teachings, making them accessible to those who might be illiterate.

3) **Architectural Symbolism:**
The architectural features of the stupa, such as its dome, harmika (square platform), chatra (ceremonial umbrella), and toranas (gateways), carry spiritual symbolism. The upward-reaching structure represents the path to enlightenment, while the harmika and chatra symbolize the elevated state of spiritual attainment.

4) **Bodhisattva Figures:**
The stupa's carvings often include depictions of Bodhisattvas, enlightened beings who delay their own liberation to help others attain enlightenment. These figures embody compassion and the ideal of selfless service to others.

D) **Influence and Legacy:**
The Amravati Stupa's influence reverberates beyond its historical context, leaving a lasting impact on various aspects:

1) **Artistic Heritage:**
The stupa's carvings and reliefs have inspired generations of artists, craftsmen, and scholars, shaping the evolution of art and aesthetics.

2) Cultural and Religious Significance:

The stupa remains a source of inspiration for understanding Buddhist philosophy, practice, and devotion. Its timeless relevance continues to resonate with seekers of wisdom and truth.

2.1.4 Sarnath Stupa:

Sarnath, a small town located near Varanasi in Uttar Pradesh, India, holds immense significance in the world of Buddhism as the place where the Buddha delivered his first sermon after attaining enlightenment. The Sarnath Stupa, also known as Dhamek Stupa, stands as a timeless symbol of this event, serving as a nexus of spirituality, history, and architectural grandeur. This stupa not only marks the beginning of the Buddhist monastic tradition but also holds within its stones the echoes of the Buddha's teachings and the evolution of Buddhist art. The Sarnath Stupa's historical significance is rooted in the life of Siddhartha Gautama, who later became the Buddha. After attaining enlightenment under the Bodhi Tree in Bodh Gaya, he journeyed to Sarnath to share his insights with his five former companions. This event, known as the First Sermon or Dhammacakkappavattana Sutta, marked the beginning of the propagation of the Four Noble Truths and the Eightfold Path.

A) Architectural Features:

The Sarnath Stupa, although having undergone multiple renovations, retains its architectural essence, which conveys the spiritual legacy of the site:

1) Shape and Structure:

The Sarnath Stupa has a cylindrical shape with a solid base and a hemispherical dome at the top. Its overall form is reminiscent of the traditional stupas found in Buddhist architecture.

2) Masonry:

The stupa's core structure is made of solid masonry, often constructed using bricks and stone. The stones might be plain or carved with decorative elements and inscriptions.

3) Dome:

The large hemispherical dome crowning the stupa symbolizes the cosmic universe and the enlightenment of Buddha. The dome is often adorned with ornamentation and sculptures, including motifs like lotus petals and medallions.

4) Harmika:

Atop the dome, there is a square platform called the harmika, which is surrounded by a railing or balustrade. The harmika represents the abode of the gods and is often adorned with symbols like the wheel of dharma or the triratna (three jewels of Buddhism).

5) Chatra:

Rising from the harmika is the chatra, a ceremonial umbrella-like structure that symbolizes high rank and honor. It is often made of multiple tiers, representing different levels of enlightenment.

B) Symbolism and Iconography:

Here are some of the prominent symbolism and iconography found in the Sarnath Stupa:

1) Wheel of Dharma:

Carvings of the Wheel of Dharma, also known as the Dharma Chakra, are often found on the stupa's harmika or the toranas (gateways). The Wheel of Dharma has eight spokes, representing the Noble Eightfold Path, which forms the core of Buddha's teachings.

2) Deer Park:

The Sarnath Stupa's role as the site of Buddha's first sermon is often illustrated through depictions of deer. Buddha's first sermon was given to his five former companions in the Deer Park at Sarnath, which is why deer are often seen in the stupa's iconography.

C) Spiritual Significance:

The Sarnath Stupa's spiritual significance transcends time and space, reflecting the core teachings of Buddhism:

1) First Sermon:

Sarnath is believed to be the place where Gautama Buddha delivered his first sermon, known as the Dhammacakkappavattana Sutta or "Setting in Motion the Wheel of Dharma." In this sermon, Buddha expounded the Four Noble Truths and the Eightfold Path, which form the core of Buddhist teachings. The site thus holds the symbolic start of the dissemination of Buddha's enlightenment and his teachings to the world.

2) Enlightenment:

The stupa represents the profound transformation and enlightenment that Gautama Buddha attained under the Bodhi tree in Bodh Gaya. The dome of the stupa, rising upwards, symbolizes the ascent from ignorance and suffering to the state of spiritual awakening and liberation.

3) Path of the Buddha:

The Sarnath Stupa serves as a tangible link to the historical Buddha. It marks a location where he walked, taught, and initiated his first disciples into the monastic order. Pilgrims visit the stupa to connect with the footsteps of Buddha and to pay homage to his teachings.

4) Pilgrimage:

The stupa is a major pilgrimage site for Buddhists from around the world. Pilgrims visit Sarnath to meditate, reflect on the teachings of Buddha, and seek spiritual solace. The presence of the stupa is a reminder of the path to enlightenment and the commitment to living a life in accordance with Buddhist principles.

5) Symbol of the Dharma:

The Sarnath Stupa represents the continuous cycle of birth, death, and rebirth (samsara) that Buddhism seeks to transcend. It also symbolizes the "Wheel of Dharma," representing the teachings of Buddha and the path to liberation from suffering.

D) Influence and Legacy:

The Sarnath Stupa's influence reverberates through time and space, impacting various facets:

1) Buddhist Philosophy:

Sarnath's teachings remain foundational to Buddhist philosophy. The First Sermon's essence continues to guide followers on the path to enlightenment.

2) Spiritual Inspiration:

The stupa's presence continues to inspire Buddhists and spiritual seekers worldwide, offering a space for reflection, meditation, and inner transformation.

2.2 Monasteries and Chaityas:

Monasteries and chaityas, integral components of ancient Indian religious architecture, embody distinct dimensions of spiritual practice, community life, and artistic expression. Monasteries, known as viharas, served as sanctuaries for Buddhist monks and nuns, fostering solitude, study, and meditation. From the austere rock-cut cells of Ajanta to the grand Nalanda University complex, viharas provided spaces for contemplation and learning, embodying the essence of the Sangha and its pursuit of enlightenment. In contrast, chaityas, or prayer halls, were designed as sacred spaces for congregational worship and communal rituals, capturing the collective spirit of devotion. The magnificent rock-cut chaityas of Karla and Bhaja, adorned with intricate sculptures and elegant arches, evoke a sense of transcendence, inviting practitioners to unite in reverence. Both monasteries and chaityas showcase exquisite architectural details - from the graceful carvings of stupas and vihara facades to the majestic horseshoe arches and prayer halls of chaityas. These architectural marvels resonate with the devotion, community, and artistry that shaped ancient Indian spiritual life, leaving an indelible mark on the evolution of religious architecture and offering modern generations a glimpse into the profound intersection of faith and creativity.

2.2.1 Monasteries in Buddhism:

Buddhism, one of the world's major religions, has a rich tradition of monasticism that dates back to the time of its founder, Siddhartha Gautama, also known as the Buddha. Monasteries play a crucial role in the practice, preservation, and propagation of Buddhist teachings and principles. In following discussion we will explore the significance of monasteries in Buddhism, their history, structure, functions, and their impact on the broader Buddhist community.

A) Monasteries (Viharas):

Monasteries in Buddhism, often referred to as "viharas," are essential institutions that play a pivotal role in preserving and propagating the teachings of the Buddha. These monastic complexes serve as sanctuaries for Buddhist monks and nuns, providing spaces for meditation, study, communal living, and the practice of the Dharma (Buddhist teachings). Monasteries hold deep spiritual significance within Buddhist traditions, serving as centers of learning, contemplation, and community for those who dedicate their lives to the pursuit of enlightenment.

B) Features of Monasteries in Buddhism:

Following are the features of monasteries in Buddhism:

1) Ascetic Living:

Buddhist monasteries are designed to facilitate the ascetic lifestyle embraced by monks and nuns. The living quarters, often called "kutis" or "cells," are intentionally kept simple to minimize material distractions and attachments, allowing monastics to focus on their spiritual practice.

2) Meditation Halls:

Monasteries feature meditation halls, known as "vihara halls," where monks and nuns gather for individual and collective meditation sessions. These halls create a conducive environment for cultivating mindfulness, mental clarity, and inner peace.

3) Scriptural Study:

Monasteries serve as centers of learning, providing monks and nuns with spaces to study Buddhist scriptures and teachings. These study sessions foster a deeper understanding of the Dharma and help monastics develop a strong foundation in Buddhist philosophy.

4) Community Spaces:

Monasteries offer communal areas where monks and nuns gather for daily activities, meals, ceremonies, and discussions. The sense of community fosters mutual support, shared learning, and a harmonious environment for spiritual growth.

C) Historical Development of Buddhist Monasteries:

The origins of Buddhist monasteries can be traced back to the time of the Buddha himself, around 6th to 5th century BCE in ancient India. After his enlightenment, the Buddha attracted a community of followers who chose to leave behind their previous lives and join him in a communal lifestyle focused on spiritual growth. This led to the formation of the first Buddhist monastic community, known as the Sangha. The Buddha provided guidelines for monastic conduct and established a code of discipline known as the Vinaya. This code outlined rules and regulations that governed the behavior of monastics and the functioning of monastic communities. The Vinaya also addressed various aspects of daily life, including etiquette, rituals, and ethical conduct.

D) Structure of Buddhist Monasteries:

Buddhist monasteries vary in size, architecture, and organization based on the cultural context and the specific Buddhist tradition they belong to. However, certain common features can be found across many monasteries:

1) Stupa or Shrine:

Monasteries often have a central stupa or shrine where relics, sacred texts, or images of the Buddha are enshrined. This serves as a focal point for devotional practices and meditation.

2) Main Hall (Dharma Hall):

This is where monastics gather for communal activities such as chanting, meditation, and teachings. It's also a place where lay Buddhists can participate in religious ceremonies.

3) Living Quarters:

Monastics reside in living quarters that may include individual cells or shared dormitories. These living spaces are designed to foster simplicity and detachment from material comforts.

4) Meditation Halls:

Monasteries often have dedicated spaces for meditation practice, reflecting the central role of meditation in Buddhist practice.

5) Library or Study Area:

Monastics engage in the study of Buddhist scriptures and philosophy, and monasteries often house libraries or study areas for this purpose.

6) Courtyard and Gardens:

Many monasteries include peaceful outdoor spaces for walking meditation and reflection.

7) Common Areas:

Monasteries have communal spaces for meals, discussions, and other interactions among monastics.

E) Functions of Monasteries in Buddhism:

Monasteries serve various important functions within the Buddhist tradition:

1) Spiritual Practice:

Monastics dedicate their lives to spiritual cultivation, including meditation, study of Buddhist teachings, and ethical development.

2) **Preservation of Dharma:**
Monasteries play a vital role in preserving and transmitting the teachings of Buddhism, including oral traditions, scriptures, and commentaries.

3) **Teaching and Guidance:**
Experienced monastics provide teachings and guidance to both fellow monastics and lay practitioners seeking spiritual advice.

4) **Community Support:**
Monasteries often engage in charitable activities, providing support to the local community through education, healthcare, and other services.

5) **Retreat and Contemplation:**
Monasteries offer a space for individuals to engage in retreats, deepening their meditation practice and self-understanding.

6) **Cultural and Artistic Preservation:**
Many monasteries house beautiful artwork, sculptures, and manuscripts that reflect the cultural and artistic heritage of the region.

F) **Famous Buddhist Monasteries:**
Following are the famous Buddhist monasteries:

1) **Nalanda University:**
Located in ancient India, Nalanda was one of the world's earliest residential universities and a renowned center of Buddhist learning. The monastery complex included lecture halls, libraries, meditation chambers, and accommodations for scholars and practitioners.

2) **Ajanta and Ellora Caves:**
These rock-cut monastic complexes in India's Maharashtra state feature intricate caves containing cells, vihara halls, and elaborate sculptures. They showcase the blend of architecture with natural landscapes and serve as significant historical and spiritual sites.

3) **Tibetan Monasteries:**
Monasteries like the Ganden Monastery and Sera Monastery in Tibet are centers of Tibetan Buddhism. They house numerous prayer halls, meditation chambers, and educational institutions, contributing to the preservation of Tibetan Buddhist teachings and culture.

G) **Legacy and Importance:**
Buddhist monasteries hold a profound legacy as spiritual centers where practitioners can dedicate their lives to the path of enlightenment. Beyond individual growth, monasteries contribute to the wider Buddhist community by preserving the teachings, nurturing spiritual leaders, and serving as beacons of wisdom and compassion. Through their commitment to meditation, ethical conduct, and the dissemination of the Dharma, these monastic institutions inspire both monastics and

laypeople to cultivate qualities that lead to inner peace, enlightenment, and the alleviation of suffering.

2.2.2 Chaityas in Jainism:

Jainism, one of the ancient spiritual traditions of India, has a rich heritage of architectural and religious structures that reflect its profound philosophy and values. Among these structures, "chaityas" hold a significant place. In following discussion we will delve into the world of chaityas in Jainism, exploring their historical development, architectural features, symbolic significance, and their role in the practice and propagation of Jain teachings.

A) Introduction to Chaityas in Jainism:

Chaityas are sacred spaces of worship, meditation, and community gathering within the Jain tradition. These structures are characterized by their distinctive architecture, which is a fusion of art, spirituality, and Jain principles. Chaityas play a vital role in promoting spiritual contemplation, fostering religious unity, and preserving Jain values and heritage.

B) Historical Development of Chaityas:

The concept of chaityas in Jainism dates back to ancient times, with roots in the life and teachings of Lord Mahavira, the 24th Tirthankara of Jainism. Jainism emerged in a socio-religious context that valued asceticism, non-violence, and introspection. As the Jain community grew, the need for communal spaces for worship, meditation, and education became apparent.

C) Architectural Features of Jain Chaityas:

Jain chaityas are characterized by their unique architectural elements, each of which holds deep symbolic significance:

1) Gavaksha or Torana:

The entrance of a Jain chaitya is often adorned with a beautifully carved gavaksha, a semi-circular arch that features intricate sculptures of auspicious symbols, Tirthankaras, celestial beings, and other spiritual motifs.

2) Pillars:

The interior of a Jain chaitya typically includes pillars that support the roof and often feature detailed carvings depicting scenes from Jain mythology, the life of Mahavira, and aspects of Jain philosophy.

3) Stupa or Image:

A stupa or an image of a Tirthankara is often the central focus of a Jain chaitya. The stupa symbolizes the attainment of nirvana by a Tirthankara, and it serves as a reminder of the ultimate goal of liberation.

4) Sculptural Details:

The walls of a Jain chaitya are adorned with sculptures that depict various Jain themes, such as the 24 Tirthankaras, scenes from the lives of saints, celestial beings, and the cycle of birth and rebirth.

D) Symbolic Significance of Jain Chaityas:

Jain chaityas are not merely architectural structures; they are repositories of deep symbolism that align with Jain principles:

1) Ahimsa (Non-Violence):

The intricate carvings and artistry within the chaityas promote a sense of reverence for all life forms, aligning with the Jain principle of non-violence.

2) Spiritual Aspiration:

The chaityas' design and embellishments inspire a sense of spiritual aspiration and reverence, inviting visitors to contemplate the path of righteousness and liberation.

3) Renunciation and Detachment:

The simplicity of the architectural design reflects the Jain ideal of renunciation and detachment from material possessions.

4) Unity and Community:

Jain chaityas provide a space for communal gatherings, promoting unity among the Jain community and fostering a sense of shared spiritual journey.

E) Role of Chaityas in Jain Practice:

Jain chaityas serve several essential roles in the practice and propagation of Jainism:

1) Worship and Meditation:

Chaityas offer a serene environment for individuals to engage in prayer, meditation, and reflection on the teachings of Jainism.

2) Education:

Chaityas often include inscriptions and sculptures that educate visitors about Jain principles, stories of Tirthankaras, and ethical values.

3) Religious Festivals:

Jain festivals and ceremonies are often conducted within the premises of chaityas, fostering a sense of community and devotion.

4) Pilgrimage Sites:

Many chaityas are located in areas of spiritual significance, becoming pilgrimage sites for Jains seeking spiritual upliftment and connection.

5) Preservation of Heritage:

The art and architecture of chaityas contribute to the preservation of Jain heritage and traditions.

F) Notable Jain Chaityas:

Following are the famous Jain chaityas:

1) **Girnar Chaitya, Gujarat:**
   The Girnar Chaitya, situated on the Girnar Mountain in Gujarat, is a significant pilgrimage site for Jains. It features a rock-cut shrine and a series of beautifully carved temples.

2) **Palitana Temples, Gujarat:**
   The Palitana temples complex comprises over 800 temples, including exquisite chaityas, atop Shatrunjaya Hill. These temples are renowned for their architectural splendor.

3) **Ranakpur Chaumukha Temple, Rajasthan:**
   This renowned marble temple features a stunning chaitya hall with intricate white marble carvings, attracting visitors with its awe-inspiring beauty.

G) Legacy and Importance:

Jain chaityas serve as vibrant centers of devotion, communal worship, and cultural preservation. These sacred spaces provide a platform for Jain devotees to express their faith, cultivate virtues, and strengthen their connection to Jain teachings. Through their artistic beauty and spiritual significance, Jain chaityas continue to inspire awe and reverence among devotees, reflecting the timeless values of Jainism and fostering a sense of unity and compassion among followers.

2.3 Painting in Buddhist and Jain Art:

Painting holds a prominent role in both Buddhist and Jain art, serving as a visual conduit for spiritual narratives and philosophical teachings. In Buddhist art, intricate thangka paintings and cave murals portray Buddha's life, Jataka tales, and meditation mandalas, guiding practitioners on paths of enlightenment. Similarly, Jain art employs illuminated manuscripts and vivid depictions of Tirthankaras to convey Jain principles of non-violence, asceticism, and liberation. Through the intricate details, rich symbolism, and vibrant colors of these paintings, both traditions offer viewers a transformative journey into the depths of their respective spiritual philosophies.

2.3.1 Painting in Buddhist Art:

Buddhism, a spiritual and philosophical tradition founded in ancient India, has given rise to a diverse and profound artistic heritage. Buddhist art serves as a visual expression of the religion's teachings, values, and spiritual insights. Within this expansive artistic landscape, painting holds a special place, encapsulating the essence of Buddhist philosophy through its imagery, symbolism, and storytelling.

A) Historical Development:

Buddhist painting has evolved over the centuries, mirroring the spread of Buddhism across different regions and cultures. Key periods in the historical development of Buddhist painting include:

1) **Early Period:**
The earliest Buddhist paintings were found in rock-cut cave temples and monasteries. These paintings depicted the life of the Buddha, Jataka tales (stories of his previous lives), and symbols such as the Wheel of Dharma. The Ajanta Caves in India are a notable example of this period.

2) **Silk Road and Central Asian Influence:**
As Buddhism spread along the Silk Road, it influenced painting styles in Central Asia, China, and beyond. The Dunhuang caves in China contain a wealth of Buddhist murals and manuscripts that highlight the cross-cultural exchanges of the time.

3) **Medieval and Himalayan Period:**
This period saw the flourishing of Buddhist painting in regions like Tibet, Nepal, and Bhutan. Thangka paintings, characterized by their intricate detail and vibrant colors, emerged as a distinctive art form, often used for meditation and teaching purposes.

4) **Japanese and Southeast Asian Influence:**
Buddhist painting took on unique regional characteristics in places like Japan and Southeast Asia. Japanese Buddhist paintings, such as the "Emaki" scrolls, used narrative storytelling to convey Buddhist teachings.

5) **Modern and Contemporary Period:**
Buddhist painting continues to evolve in the modern era, influenced by changing artistic styles and societal shifts. Contemporary artists fuse traditional techniques with modern interpretations, creating a dynamic and evolving landscape of Buddhist art.

B) **Themes and Iconography:**
Buddhist painting encompasses a wide range of themes and iconographic motifs, each carrying deep spiritual significance. Some of the prominent themes include:

1) **Life of the Buddha**:
Scenes from the life of Siddhartha Gautama, from his birth to his enlightenment and subsequent teachings, are frequently depicted in Buddhist painting. These scenes emphasize key events that illustrate the path to enlightenment.

2) **Jataka Tales**:
Jataka tales recount the past lives of the Buddha, illustrating moral lessons and virtues. These tales often involve animals and humans and offer teachings on compassion, generosity, and ethical conduct.

3) **Bodhisattvas and Deities**:
Bodhisattvas, enlightened beings who postpone their own liberation to assist others, are central figures in Buddhist painting. Deities like Avalokiteshvara, Tara, and Manjushri embody various qualities and virtues, inspiring devotion and spiritual growth.

4) Mandalas and Cosmology:

Mandalas are intricate geometric designs that symbolize the universe and its various realms. Mandalas are used in Vajrayana Buddhism as aids in meditation, guiding practitioners toward spiritual realization.

5) Pure Lands and Paradises:

Some Buddhist traditions emphasize the concept of "Pure Lands" or paradises where beings can attain enlightenment. Paintings of these paradises depict serene landscapes inhabited by enlightened beings.

C) Styles and Techniques:

Buddhist painting showcases a diverse array of styles and techniques that have evolved across different cultures and historical periods:

1) Indian and Gandharan Styles:

Early Buddhist paintings in India and the Gandharan region often incorporated Greco-Roman artistic elements. These styles focused on naturalistic representations of the Buddha and other figures.

2) Chinese Ink Painting:

Chinese Buddhist painting, influenced by Daoist aesthetics, emphasizes the use of ink and brushwork. This style conveys a sense of fluidity and spontaneity, mirroring the impermanence inherent in Buddhist philosophy.

3) Tibetan Thangka Painting:

Thangka paintings are central to Tibetan Buddhist art. These intricate scrolls often depict deities, mandalas, and religious narratives. Thangkas are used in rituals, meditation, and teaching contexts.

4) Japanese Emaki Scrolls:

Japanese Buddhist painting in the form of emaki scrolls employs narrative storytelling to convey Buddhist teachings. These scrolls often unfold horizontally, offering a sequential visual experience.

5) Contemporary Innovations:

Modern Buddhist artists blend traditional techniques with contemporary aesthetics. This fusion allows for creative expressions that resonate with contemporary audiences while staying true to the essence of Buddhist teachings.

D) Spiritual Significance:

Buddhist painting transcends mere aesthetic appreciation; it serves as a powerful medium for spiritual contemplation and education. Its significance within Buddhism can be understood through various aspects:

1) Visual Dharma:

Buddhist paintings are considered a form of "visual Dharma" – a means of conveying the teachings of Buddhism. They offer accessible ways for individuals, including those who might be illiterate, to engage with and internalize the teachings.

2) **Meditative Aid**:
The intricate details, vibrant colors, and symbolism in Buddhist paintings serve as focal points for meditation. Practitioners use paintings to direct their minds toward specific qualities, virtues, or teachings.

3) **Devotional Practice**:
Paintings of Buddhas, Bodhisattvas, and deities inspire devotion and reverence. Devotees create personal connections with these figures, seeking their guidance and blessings on their spiritual journey.

4) **Karmic Merit**:
The creation and sponsorship of Buddhist paintings are considered acts of merit in many Buddhist traditions. This act of generosity is believed to contribute to positive karmic accumulation.

5) **Cultural and Historical Preservation**:
Buddhist paintings serve as repositories of cultural heritage, preserving not only religious teachings but also historical and artistic achievements.

2.3.2 Painting in Jain Art:

Jainism, one of the oldest religions of India, has a rich artistic tradition that spans centuries. Central to Jain art is the concept of non-violence (ahimsa), compassion, and the pursuit of spiritual purity. Jain painting, an integral component of Jain art, has a unique and profound visual language that reflects the core principles and philosophy of the religion.

A) Historical Development:

Jain painting has its roots in ancient India and evolved over various periods, drawing inspiration from diverse sources such as religious texts, philosophical tenets, and cultural influences. The following periods are notable in the historical development of Jain painting:

1) **Ancient Period (circa 1st to 6th centuries CE)**:
Early Jain paintings were predominantly found in rock-cut cave temples and monuments. These paintings were characterized by their simplicity, using vibrant colors and basic forms to depict Jain Tirthankaras (spiritual teachers), yakshas, and yakshis (celestial beings).

2) **Medieval Period (circa 7th to 12th centuries CE)**:
During this period, Jain painting began to flourish with the creation of illustrated manuscripts and palm-leaf manuscripts. These manuscripts depicted Jain cosmology, sacred texts, and the lives of Tirthankaras through intricate miniatures. The Digambara and Shwetambara sects each developed distinct styles, with the former favoring minimalist depictions and the latter embracing more ornate and detailed representations.

3) **Rajput Period (circa 15th to 19th centuries CE)**:
Jain painting received patronage from Rajput rulers, leading to the creation of lavish manuscripts and wall paintings. These works often incorporated elements of courtly aesthetics while retaining the essence of Jain philosophy. The Rajput courts were responsible for commissioning illustrated versions of Jain texts such as the Kalpasutra and Kalakacharya Katha.

4) **Modern Period (19th century onwards)**:
The influence of Western art and colonialism led to a decline in traditional Jain painting. However, some artists continued to produce works in the traditional style, often using new mediums and techniques. Jain themes were also incorporated into modern art movements, contributing to the continuation of Jain artistic expressions.

B) **Themes and Iconography:**
Jain painting is characterized by its unique themes and iconography that revolve around Jain philosophy, ethics, and cosmology. Some prominent themes include:

1) **Tirthankaras and Their Lives**:
Jain paintings often depict the lives and teachings of the Tirthankaras, who are revered as enlightened beings. These paintings emphasize their virtues, spiritual journey, and the events of their lives, symbolizing the path to liberation.

2) **Yakshas and Yakshis**:
Celestial beings known as yakshas and yakshis are an integral part of Jain mythology. Depicted as benevolent guardians, they are often portrayed in Jain paintings as powerful and graceful figures, reflecting the Jain ideals of balance and harmony.

3) **Jain Cosmology**:
Jainism has a complex cosmological worldview that includes various realms and states of existence. Jain paintings illustrate this cosmology, depicting the cycle of birth, death, and rebirth (samsara), as well as the ultimate goal of liberation (moksha).

4) **Austere Aesthetics**:
Jain art emphasizes simplicity and restraint. Many Jain paintings exude a sense of asceticism, with minimalist backgrounds and subdued colors that reflect the practice of non-attachment and renunciation.

C) **Styles and Techniques:**
Jain painting exhibits a diverse range of styles and techniques that have evolved over time. Some notable styles include:

1) **Sculptural Style**:
Early Jain paintings were influenced by the sculptural traditions of the time. The figures in these paintings often had a three-dimensional quality, resembling the sculptures found in Jain temples and monuments.

2) **Miniature Painting**:
The medieval period saw the emergence of miniature painting in Jain manuscripts. These miniatures were characterized by intricate detailing, vibrant colors, and intricate patterns, creating a visual spectacle that complemented the textual content.

3) **Courtly Style**:
During the Rajput period, Jain painting was influenced by the courtly aesthetics of the ruling dynasties. This style often incorporated luxurious details and elaborate ornamentation, reflecting the opulence of the courts.

4) **Contemporary Expressions**:
In the modern period, artists experimented with new techniques and mediums, adapting Jain themes to contemporary art forms. While retaining the essence of Jain philosophy, these artists brought a fresh perspective to Jain painting.

D) **Spiritual Significance:**
Jain painting goes beyond mere artistic expression; it serves as a visual medium for spiritual contemplation and education. Its significance within Jainism can be understood through the following aspects:

1) **Dharma Teaching**:
Jain paintings encapsulate the core principles of Jain dharma, acting as teaching tools that convey the intricacies of Jain philosophy to both the learned and the layperson.

2) **Spiritual Inspiration**:
Jain paintings inspire devotion and reverence among practitioners, reminding them of the path of non-violence, truth, and compassion that leads to spiritual liberation.

3) **Meditative Focus**:
The intricate details and symbolism in Jain paintings provide a focal point for meditation, aiding practitioners in their contemplative practices and helping them internalize Jain teachings.

4) **Cultural Heritage**:
Jain painting preserves the cultural heritage of the religion, reflecting the deep connection between art and spirituality in Jain society.

♦♦♦

Review Questions

Q.1. Answer the Following Questions:

1) Explain in detail about the Sanchi Stupa.
2) Discuss about the Bharhut Stupa.
3) Explain about the Amravati Stupa.
4) Explain in detail about the Sarnath Stupa.
5) Discuss about the Monasteries in Buddhism.
6) Explain in detail about the Chaityas in Jainism.
7) Explain the Painting in Buddhist Art.
8) Discuss about the Painting in Jain Art.

Q.3. Write Short Notes on:

a) Sanchi Stupa
b) Bharhut Stupa
c) Amravati Stupa
d) Sarnath Stupa
e) Features of Monasteries.
f) Features of Chaityas.
g) Painting in Buddhist Art.
h) Painting in Jain Art.

♦♦♦

UNIT 3

Sculptures, Painting & Rock - Cut Architecture in India

Introduction:

India's artistic heritage thrives in the intricate triad of sculpture, painting, and rock-cut architecture, each form an illuminating chapter in the country's cultural narrative. Sculpture, a timeless medium, embodies spiritual beliefs and cultural expressions with its symbolic iconography and regional diversity, adorning temples and ancient sites alike. Meanwhile, painting, from the ancient cave murals of Ajanta to the opulent miniatures of the Mughal era, captures history and spirituality on canvas, creating vivid visual narratives that endure through time. Complementing these, India's rock-cut architecture chisels stories into the very bedrock, from the awe-inspiring temples of Ellora and Elephanta to the monolithic splendor of the Kailasa Temple, revealing the remarkable human ability to transform stone into sacred sanctuaries, all three forms together forming a multifaceted testament to India's artistic and cultural legacy.

3.1 Bhimbetka:

The Bhimbetka Rock Shelters, ensconced in the Vindhya mountain range of Madhya Pradesh, India, represent an extraordinary archaeological treasure trove, offering a captivating glimpse into the world of our prehistoric ancestors. Designated as a UNESCO World Heritage Site, the Bhimbetka caves bear a testament to the creativity, cultural practices & artistic prowess of early humans over a span of thousands of years.

A) Archeological Significance:

Here are some key aspects of Bhimbetka's archaeological significance:

1) Chronological Depth:

The rock art found at Bhimbetka spans an impressive timespan, ranging from the Paleolithic era (around 10,000 years ago) to the historic period. This extended chronology allows archaeologists to observe and study the gradual changes in human behavior, lifestyle, and artistic styles over millennia.

2) **Visual Documentation of Prehistoric Life:**

The intricate rock paintings offer a visual record of the lives, beliefs, and activities of early human societies. Scenes of hunting, gathering, dancing, communal activities, and rituals provide insights into the day-to-day existence of these ancient communities.

3) **Cultural Evolution and Adaptation:**

The changing themes and motifs in the rock art reflect the cultural evolution of human societies. From simple geometric patterns in the Paleolithic to more complex and narrative scenes in later periods, Bhimbetka's art mirrors the progression from nomadic hunting-gathering to settled agricultural lifestyles.

4) **Socioeconomic Insights:**

The art at Bhimbetka allows researchers to infer aspects of the economic and social systems of the past. Depictions of hunting scenes, domesticated animals, and communal activities provide clues about subsistence strategies, division of labor, and community organization.

5) **Spiritual and Ritualistic Practices:**

Many interpretations of the rock art suggest that they could have had ritualistic or ceremonial significance. Images of animals, humans, and abstract symbols might have held symbolic meanings related to religious or shamanistic practices, offering a glimpse into the spiritual world of prehistoric humans.

6) **Cultural Continuity and Change:**

The superimposition of different layers of paintings on the same rock surfaces illustrates the continuity and changes in cultural practices over time. This phenomenon allows researchers to trace shifts in artistic styles, symbolism, and cultural motifs.

7) **Technological Advancements:**

The rock art also provides insights into the technological advancements of the time. Changes in tools and pigments used for painting can be observed, reflecting shifts in available resources and artistic techniques.

8) **Human-Environment Interaction:**

The depiction of flora and fauna in the paintings offers information about the environment and climatic conditions during different periods. This enables researchers to reconstruct past landscapes and ecosystems and understand how humans interacted with their surroundings.

B) **Rock Art & its Varieties:**

Here are some of the notable varieties of rock art found at Bhimbetka:

1) **Paleolithic Geometric Art:**
The oldest paintings at Bhimbetka, dating back around 10,000 years, consist of simple geometric patterns. These patterns, often created using red and white pigments, include lines, dots, zigzags, and grids. While their exact meanings are open to interpretation, they might have held symbolic or ritualistic significance.

2) **Animals and Hunting Scenes:**
As time progressed, the paintings started depicting animals and hunting scenes. These artworks offer insights into the importance of hunting in the lives of these early communities. Animals such as bisons, deer, tigers, and elephants are depicted, possibly symbolizing the close relationship between humans and the natural world.

3) **Dancing and Ritualistic Figures:**
The Mesolithic and Chalcolithic periods brought a shift toward more complex and narrative art. Paintings of dancing figures, often depicted in groups, suggest communal activities or rituals. These scenes might provide glimpses into the social and spiritual aspects of prehistoric life.

4) **Daily Life and Communal Activities:**
The paintings also capture scenes from everyday life, portraying activities like cooking, gathering, and interacting with animals. These depictions offer insights into the subsistence strategies and social dynamics of early human societies.

5) **Cultural Symbolism and Rituals:**
Some paintings feature abstract symbols and signs that could represent cultural symbols or rituals. These symbols might have held spiritual or communicative significance within the community.

6) **Handprints and Stencils:**
Handprints and stencils are a distinctive feature of Bhimbetka's rock art. These imprints might have served as a form of artistic expression or as a way to leave a mark, symbolizing the presence of individuals or groups.

7) **Mythological and Narrative Art:**
A later phase of Bhimbetka's art includes depictions of more complex narratives, often involving humans and animals. These scenes could potentially represent mythological stories or legends that were passed down through generations.

8) **Superimposed Layers:**
Over time, multiple layers of paintings were created on the same surfaces, leading to a palimpsest effect. This phenomenon offers a unique opportunity to observe the evolution of artistic styles and themes within a single shelter.

C) **Interpretive Challenges:**
Following are the interpretive challenges of bhimbetka rock art:

1) **Symbolic Ambiguity:**
Perhaps the most significant challenge in interpreting Bhimbetka's rock art lies in the ambiguity of its symbols and motifs. The visual language employed by the ancient artists might be vastly different from modern iconography. The same symbol could have held various meanings, depending on context, culture, and intent. Deciphering the inherent symbolism requires bridging the cognitive and emotional landscapes of two different eras.

2) **Cultural Context:**
The chasm of time that separates us from the creators of the rock art poses a considerable challenge. The cultural context that informed the creation of the art has been lost to the ages. The beliefs, rituals, and societal structures of those times were distinct from our own, making it challenging to understand the motivations and meanings behind the art from a contemporary standpoint.

3) **Subjectivity and Bias:**
Interpreting Bhimbetka's art involves a subjective journey that can be influenced by the biases, perspectives, and cultural frameworks of modern researchers. The symbols and scenes may evoke different emotions and meanings for different individuals, leading to a diverse array of interpretations. The challenge lies in minimizing the imposition of present-day viewpoints onto the ancient canvas.

4) **Shifting Symbolism:**
Symbols and motifs used in the rock art might have evolved over time, reflecting changes in cultural practices and belief systems. This shifting symbolism complicates interpretation, as a symbol that represented one thing in an earlier era might have taken on a different connotation in subsequent periods.

5) **Lack of Contemporary Records:**
Unlike historical periods with written records, Bhimbetka's creators left no explanations or written documentation of their art. This absence of direct commentary on the meaning of the art means that researchers must rely on contextual clues, comparative studies, and cross-cultural analyses to piece together possible interpretations.

6) **Multifunctionality of Art:**
The rock art at Bhimbetka might have served multiple functions, from ritualistic and ceremonial to narrative and aesthetic. Determining the primary intent behind a particular painting can be challenging due to the multifaceted nature of the art and the varying roles it might have played within the community.

7) **Loss of Cultural Memory:**
Over the millennia, the original meanings and interpretations of symbols and scenes could have been lost. The oral traditions that could have passed down the stories behind the art might have faded away, leaving behind a visual record that is cryptic and mysterious.

8) **Preservation and Deterioration:**

The condition of the rock art itself presents challenges. Weathering, erosion, and human activity have led to the degradation of some paintings. This deterioration can erase subtle details and obscure the intentions of the ancient artists, making accurate interpretation even more difficult.

3.2 Bagh, Ajanta, Ellora & Tanjore:

The cultural tapestry of India is woven with the splendid threads of Bagh's ancient Gupta-period wall paintings, illuminating Buddhist narratives with vibrant colors; the intricate frescoes and sculptures of Ajanta's rock-cut caves, spanning centuries and revealing the spiritual devotion of Buddhism; the awe-inspiring rock-cut architecture of Ellora's diverse cave complex, where Hindu, Buddhist, and Jain expressions converge in magnificent monolithic forms; and the resplendent temples of Tanjore, epitomizing Chola dynasty's architectural brilliance and artistic finesse, crafting a profound narrative of India's historical, artistic, and religious continuum.

3.2.1 Bagh Caves:

The Bagh Caves, a group of ancient rock-cut caves in central India, are a testament to the rich artistic and religious heritage of the region. These caves, located near the village of Bagh in the Dhar district of Madhya Pradesh, hold a significant place in the history of Indian art and architecture. In following discussion we will explore the history, architecture, art, and cultural significance of the Bagh Caves.

A) **Introduction:**

The Bagh Caves are a group of nine rock-cut caves carved into a hillside, dating back to the 5th to 7th centuries CE. These caves showcase intricate carvings, sculptures, and frescoes that reflect the religious and cultural life of the time. The caves are primarily associated with the Buddhist faith, showcasing the devotion of the artists and the people of the region.

B) **Historical Background:**

The period during which the Bagh Caves were created was marked by a flourishing of art, culture, and spirituality in India. The Gupta Empire had laid the foundation for a golden era of artistic expression, and the subsequent centuries saw the continuation of these creative endeavors under different dynasties.

C) **Architecture and Layout:**

The Bagh Caves are primarily Buddhist in nature and follow the traditional layout of rock-cut caves found in India. Each cave consists of a sanctum, a pillared hall, and an open courtyard. The sanctum typically housed a stupa, representing the enlightened mind of the Buddha, while the hall provided space for communal gatherings and worship.

D) Artistic Marvels:

The true splendor of the Bagh Caves lies in their artistic treasures, which include sculptures, carvings, and exquisite frescoes:

1) Sculptures:

The caves are adorned with sculptures depicting various aspects of Buddhist iconography, including images of the Buddha, bodhisattvas, and scenes from the life of the Buddha. The artists skillfully rendered these figures, capturing the spiritual serenity and compassion associated with Buddhist teachings.

2) Frescoes:

The Bagh Caves are renowned for their vibrant frescoes that cover the walls and ceilings of some of the caves. These frescoes depict scenes from Jataka tales (stories of the Buddha's previous lives), mythical creatures, celestial beings, and other elements of Buddhist cosmology.

3) Carvings:

The intricately carved doorways, pillars, and panels in the caves showcase the artistic finesse of the craftsmen. These carvings often feature delicate floral motifs, geometric patterns, and depictions of lotus flowers and other symbols.

E) Cultural and Religious Significance:

The Bagh Caves hold immense cultural and religious significance:

1) Spiritual Retreat:

The caves served as spaces for Buddhist monks and practitioners to engage in meditation, reflection, and religious practices. The serene environment of the caves facilitated a deep connection with the teachings of the Buddha.

2) Religious Devotion:

The artistic expressions found in the caves reflect the devotion and reverence of the artists and the people who frequented the caves. These expressions of faith served as a source of inspiration and a reminder of the spiritual path.

3) Teaching Through Art:

The frescoes and sculptures acted as visual aids for conveying Buddhist teachings and stories to both monks and lay devotees.

4) Artistic Legacy:

The Bagh Caves stand as a testament to the artistic brilliance of ancient Indian craftsmen. They provide insights into the aesthetic sensibilities, technical skills, and cultural values of the time.

F) Preservation and Conservation:

Over the centuries, the Bagh Caves faced challenges due to natural elements, human activities, and neglect. However, efforts by archaeological and cultural organizations have been directed toward their preservation and conservation. Conservation measures include cleaning, restoration of damaged artwork, and the implementation of visitor management strategies to ensure the continued protection of these treasures.

G) Contemporary Significance:

The Bagh Caves continue to draw scholars, researchers, and tourists from around the world. They offer a window into the artistic achievements of ancient India and provide insights into the cultural and spiritual life of the people who inhabited the region centuries ago. The caves also contribute to the understanding of the evolution of Indian art and its influences.

3.2.2 Ajanta Caves:

The Ajanta Caves, a magnificent complex of rock-cut Buddhist cave temples, hold an exceptional place in the history of art, architecture, and religious devotion. Nestled in the rugged hills of Maharashtra, India, these caves have captivated the imagination of people worldwide for their intricate sculptures, exquisite paintings, and profound spiritual significance. In following discussion we will explore the historical context, architectural features, artistic treasures, religious significance, and enduring legacy of the Ajanta Caves.

A) Introduction:

The Ajanta Caves are a UNESCO World Heritage Site that comprises a series of 30 rock-cut cave temples, monasteries, and chaityas (prayer halls) hewn into the cliffside of the Waghora River valley. Dating back to the 2nd century BCE to the 5th century CE, the caves are a remarkable testament to the artistic achievements and spiritual devotion of ancient India.

B) Historical Context:

The caves were created during a period of significant historical and cultural development. The early caves were built under the patronage of the Mauryan and Satavahana dynasties, and later caves were constructed under the Vakataka dynasty. These dynasties were influenced by Buddhism, and their support contributed to the flourishing of Buddhist art and architecture.

C) Architectural and Layout Features:

The Ajanta Caves are divided into two groups: the earlier Hinayana caves (Caves 9, 10, 12, 13, and 15A) and the later Mahayana caves (the rest). The caves share common architectural elements:

1) Chaityas (Prayer Halls):

The earlier caves feature chaityas, characterized by a stupa at the center and a semi-circular apse. These were spaces for congregational worship.

2) Viharas (Monasteries):

The later caves consist of viharas, with a central hall for communal activities and individual cells for monks to meditate and reside.

3) Stupas and Pillars:
Stupas were often placed within the chaityas and viharas, symbolizing the presence of the Buddha. Elaborately carved pillars supported the structures and were adorned with intricate designs.

D) Artistic Treasures:
The Ajanta Caves are renowned for their artistic excellence, including both sculptures and paintings:

1) Sculptures:
Intricately carved sculptures adorn the facades and interiors of the caves. These sculptures depict various figures from Buddhist cosmology, including the Buddha, bodhisattvas, attendants, and celestial beings.

2) Paintings:
The most celebrated feature of the Ajanta Caves is their vivid frescoes. These paintings, executed on the cave walls, depict scenes from the life of the Buddha, Jataka tales, and other religious narratives. The use of vibrant colors and meticulous detailing showcases the mastery of ancient Indian artists.

E) Religious Significance:
The Ajanta Caves are deeply significant in the context of Buddhism:

1) Spiritual Practice:
The caves provided a conducive environment for Buddhist monks to meditate, reflect, and engage in religious practices.

2) Teaching and Contemplation:
The paintings and sculptures served as visual aids for conveying Buddhist teachings, stories, and moral lessons to both monks and laypeople.

3) Devotion and Inspiration:
The art and architecture of the caves inspired devotion and facilitated a connection between the material and the spiritual realms.

4) Cultural Exchange:
The diverse range of artistic styles and influences seen in the paintings and sculptures highlight the cultural exchange between different regions and periods.

F) Legacy and Rediscovery:
The Ajanta Caves were abandoned in the 7th century CE due to a variety of factors, including the decline of Buddhism in India and the shifting political landscape. The caves remained hidden from the world until their rediscovery by a British officer, John Smith, in 1819. Their rediscovery sparked a renewed interest in Indian art and history.

G) Preservation and Tourism:
In recognition of their immense cultural value, the Ajanta Caves were designated as a UNESCO World Heritage Site in 1983. Conservation efforts have been ongoing to

protect and preserve the fragile paintings and sculptures from the effects of time, weather, and tourism. The introduction of controlled visitor access has helped strike a balance between sharing these treasures with the world and ensuring their long-term survival.

H) Contemporary Significance:

The Ajanta Caves continue to inspire awe and wonder in people from all walks of life. They serve as a testament to the artistic genius, spiritual devotion, and cultural exchange that characterized ancient India. The caves also contribute to contemporary discussions on the preservation of cultural heritage and the role of art in conveying profound philosophical and spiritual concepts.

3.2.3 Ellora Caves:

The Ellora Caves, an awe-inspiring complex of rock-cut temples and monasteries, constitute one of India's most remarkable architectural and artistic achievements. Nestled in the Deccan plateau of Maharashtra, these caves showcase a harmonious blend of Hindu, Buddhist, and Jain traditions, offering a glimpse into the cultural, religious, and artistic diversity of ancient India. In following discussion we will delve into the historical context, architectural features, artistic treasures, religious significance, and lasting impact of the Ellora Caves.

A) Introduction:

The Ellora Caves form a UNESCO World Heritage Site consisting of 34 rock-cut caves adorned with sculptures, paintings, and architectural marvels. Spanning a period from the 6th to the 10th century CE, these caves are an embodiment of the creative spirit and spiritual devotion that flourished in the heart of the Deccan region.

B) Historical Context:

The Ellora Caves were created during a dynamic period of Indian history, marked by the rise and fall of various dynasties and the confluence of different religious traditions. Dynasties such as the Rashtrakutas, Chalukyas, and Yadavas played a pivotal role in the patronage and development of the caves.

C) Architectural Diversity:

The Ellora Caves are organized into three groups: the Buddhist caves, the Hindu caves, and the Jain caves. This diversity reflects the pluralistic nature of ancient Indian society and the coexistence of various religious beliefs.

1) Buddhist Caves (Caves 1-12):

The Buddhist caves predominantly represent the Theravada tradition. They include monasteries, chaityas (prayer halls), and viharas (monastic residences) that exemplify the serene simplicity of Buddhist architecture.

2) Hindu Caves (Caves 13-29):

The Hindu caves showcase intricate carvings and sculptures dedicated to various deities. The Kailasa Temple (Cave 16) stands out as a stunning architectural masterpiece, dedicated to Lord Shiva.

3) Jain Caves (Caves 30-34):

The Jain caves, reflecting the principles of Jainism, feature sculptures of Tirthankaras (spiritual teachers) and intricate detailing that highlight Jain aesthetics.

D) Artistic Splendor:

The artistic wonders of the Ellora Caves encompass sculptures, carvings, and paintings that illuminate the walls and interiors of these ancient sanctuaries:

1) Sculptures:

The caves are adorned with intricate sculptures depicting gods, goddesses, celestial beings, and mythological narratives. The life-like renderings reflect the exceptional skill of the craftsmen.

2) Carvings:

The caves boast meticulously carved panels and pillars adorned with ornate designs, showcasing the technical prowess and creative imagination of the artisans.

3) Paintings:

While the paintings in the Ellora Caves are not as extensive as those in Ajanta, remnants of murals can still be found. These fragments offer glimpses into the vibrant colors and themes that once adorned the cave interiors.

E) Religious Significance:

The Ellora Caves hold profound religious and spiritual significance:

1) Spiritual Sanctuary:

The caves served as sanctuaries for spiritual practice, offering monks, devotees, and pilgrims spaces for worship, meditation, and contemplation.

2) Cultural Exchange:

The coexistence of different religious traditions within a single complex reflects the spirit of tolerance, dialogue, and exchange that characterized ancient India.

3) Art as a Spiritual Expression:

The artistic creations within the caves transcend mere decoration; they convey the deep devotion and reverence of both artists and patrons.

F) Legacy and Rediscovery:

The Ellora Caves, much like the Ajanta Caves, fell into obscurity after the decline of their patronizing dynasties. Rediscovered by the British in the 19th century, they captured the imagination of scholars, artists, and historians, prompting renewed interest in India's rich cultural heritage.

G) Contemporary Relevance:

The Ellora Caves continue to resonate with people across the globe:

1) **Cultural Heritage:**

They offer insights into the multi-layered cultural heritage of India, fostering an appreciation for its artistic and spiritual legacy.

2) **Interfaith Dialogue:**

The coexistence of diverse religious traditions within the caves invites reflection on interfaith harmony and mutual respect.

3) **Inspiration:**

The artistry and devotion evident in the caves inspire contemporary artists, architects, and seekers to explore the interplay between creativity and spirituality.

3.2.4 Tanjore Caves:

In the heartland of Tamil Nadu, India lays Tanjore (Thanjavur), a city synonymous with Chola dynasty's architectural magnificence and artistic finesse. Revered for its monumental temples and intricate sculptures, Tanjore's rock-cut architecture embodies the zenith of Chola artistic brilliance. The Brihadeeswara Temple, an iconic UNESCO World Heritage Site, stands as a testament to the architectural grandeur, cultural legacy, and spiritual devotion that defined the Chola era.

1) **Historical Legacy of the Chola Dynasty:**

Tanjore rose to prominence during the Chola dynasty's reign, a period marked by political stability, economic prosperity, and cultural flowering. The Cholas left an indelible mark on South Indian art, architecture, and governance, and the Brihadeeswara Temple stands as a beacon of their artistic legacy.

2) **The Brihadeeswara Temple:**

A Marvel in Stone: The Brihadeeswara Temple, constructed under the patronage of Chola emperor Rajaraja I in the 11th century CE, is a paragon of Dravidian architecture. Often referred to as the "Big Temple," its colossal vimana (tower) dominates the landscape and represents the zenith of Chola architectural ingenuity.

3) **Architectural Features:**

The temple's architectural layout follows the Dravidian style, characterized by pyramidal towers, ornate pillars, and intricately carved sculptures. The temple complex includes a sanctum, a mandapa (assembly hall), and a towering vimana, all meticulously designed with mathematical precision.

4) **Sculptural Splendor:**

The Brihadeeswara Temple is adorned with exquisite sculptures that narrate Hindu mythological narratives, depict deities, and showcase the socio-religious life of the Chola period. The sculptures exhibit an impeccable attention to detail and artistic finesse.

5) **Cosmic Symbolism and Spiritual Significance:**
The architecture of the Brihadeeswara Temple is infused with cosmic symbolism and spiritual significance. The vimana represents Mount Meru, the abode of the gods, while the intricate sculptures communicate philosophical concepts and narratives from Hindu epics.

6) **Rajaraja Chola's Vision:**
Emperor Rajaraja-I's vision for the temple extended beyond its architectural grandeur. The temple was not only a place of worship but also a cultural center, fostering art, music, dance, and scholarly pursuits.

7) **UNESCO Recognition and Conservation:**
The Brihadeeswara Temple's exceptional cultural significance led to its recognition as a UNESCO World Heritage Site in 1987. Conservation efforts have been undertaken to protect its stone carvings, murals, and structural integrity.

8) **Enduring Cultural Legacy:**
Tanjore's architectural legacy reverberates through time, inspiring generations to appreciate the architectural prowess of the Chola dynasty. The temple continues to be a place of worship, drawing pilgrims and enthusiasts from around the world.

9) **Tanjore Bronzes:**
Sculptural Marvels: Tanjore is also renowned for its intricate bronze sculptures that blend aesthetic beauty with religious devotion. These sculptures, often depicting Hindu deities, exemplify the Chola era's artistic sensibilities.

10) **Influence on Contemporary Art:**
The artistic legacy of Tanjore extends beyond its historical era. The Chola style of art and architecture has inspired contemporary artists, continuing to shape South Indian artistic expressions.

3.3 Symbolism of Temple Architecture:

Temple architecture has been a prominent and enduring cultural phenomenon throughout human history. Temples serve as physical embodiments of religious and spiritual beliefs, acting as sacred spaces where devotees connect with the divine. Beyond their functional aspects, temples often carry profound symbolism in their design, layout, and ornamentation. This symbolism varies across cultures, religions, and historical periods, reflecting the unique worldviews and cosmologies of each society.

A) **Historical Context**
The roots of temple architecture can be traced back to ancient civilizations, where they were erected to honor deities, commemorate important events, or facilitate rituals. From the colossal temples of ancient Egypt to the intricate pagodas of East Asia, these structures encapsulated the prevailing beliefs and values of their respective societies. Throughout history, temple architecture often embodied the

synthesis of religion, art, and architecture, reflecting the interconnectedness of these disciplines.

B) Architectural Elements as Symbols:

The architecture of temples is a visual language through which intricate symbolism is conveyed. Every aspect of a temple's design, from its layout to its decorative elements, carries profound meanings that reflect the spiritual, cultural, and societal values of the civilization that built it.

1) Layout and Orientation:

The layout and orientation of a temple are not arbitrary choices; they hold deep symbolic significance. Many temples are aligned with celestial phenomena, cardinal directions, or geographical features. For instance, Hindu temples are often oriented toward the east, where the sun rises, signifying the dawn of knowledge and enlightenment. The alignment with specific celestial events emphasizes the connection between the earthly realm and the cosmic order.

2) Axis Mundi:

The concept of the axis mundi, or the cosmic axis, is a central theme in temple architecture. Temples are often designed to represent the axis that connects different realms earth, heavens, and the underworld. The temple's main axis, often visible in its central hallway or tower, serves as a conduit for spiritual energy to flow between these realms. This vertical axis symbolizes the connection between the material and spiritual dimensions, and the journey of the soul towards higher states of consciousness.

3) Sacred Geometry:

Sacred geometry, a set of geometric ratios and proportions believed to possess inherent spiritual significance, is integrated into temple architecture. The application of sacred geometry creates harmonious and balanced spaces that resonate with cosmic order. The use of geometric shapes, such as circles and squares, in the layout and design of temples aligns the physical space with universal principles and underlying truths.

4) Symbolic Elements:

The intricate details of temple architecture, including sculptures, carvings, and reliefs, are rich with symbolism. Each decorative element tells a story or imparts a message. These elements often depict deities, mythological narratives, and cosmic themes. For example, the depiction of gods and goddesses in specific poses or gestures communicates their attributes and qualities. Animals, plants, and geometric patterns are also woven into the design, representing the interconnectedness of all life and the divine order of creation.

5) Elements of Transition:

Transition zones within temple architecture, such as gateways, doorways, and thresholds, hold symbolic significance. Crossing these thresholds is often seen as moving from the mundane world to the sacred realm. The lintel above a temple entrance might be adorned with sculptures representing guardians or divine protectors, signifying the boundary between the secular and spiritual domains.

6) **Vertical Ascent:**

In many temple designs, there is a deliberate progression from lower to higher levels. Climbing stairs or ascending through multiple tiers signifies the soul's journey towards spiritual enlightenment. This vertical movement symbolizes the ascent from the material world to the divine realm, with each level representing a higher state of consciousness.

7) **Elements of Nature:**

Elements of nature, such as water features, trees, and gardens, are often incorporated into temple complexes. These natural elements carry symbolic meanings water symbolizes purification and renewal, while trees represent growth and the interconnectedness of life. The integration of nature into temple architecture harmonizes the built environment with the natural world, reinforcing the idea of unity between humanity and the cosmos.

C) **Religious Symbolism:**

Religious symbolism is at the heart of temple architecture, as these structures are primarily erected to honor and facilitate the worship of deities and spiritual beings. Every facet of temple design, from its layout to its decorative elements, is imbued with religious meanings that reflect the beliefs, rituals, and cosmology of the specific faith.

1) **Deity Representation:**

Central to temple architecture is the representation of deities and divine beings. These representations are not merely artistic renditions but serve as focal points for devotion and worship. The way deities are depicted through sculptures, paintings, or idols carries deep religious symbolism. Their poses, gestures, and attributes convey their qualities and roles within the spiritual tradition.

2) **Cosmic Symbolism:**

Temples often embody the cosmological beliefs of a particular religion. The layout and architecture of the temple may mirror the structure of the universe as described in religious texts. The divisions within the temple, such as the sanctum sanctorum and various chambers, can symbolize different cosmic realms. The vertical ascent within the temple signifies the soul's journey from the material plane to the divine sphere.

3) **Ritual Symbolism:**

Temples are designed to facilitate specific rituals and ceremonies integral to the religious practice. The layout and arrangement of spaces guide worshippers through prescribed rituals, creating a sense of spiritual engagement and connection with the divine. Elements like altars, fire pits, and water features hold ritualistic significance, serving as mediums for communication with the divine.

4) **Symbolic Geometry:**
The use of geometric patterns and proportions in temple architecture often carries religious symbolism. Circles, squares, and mandalas can represent cosmic order and unity. For example, the mandala a geometric symbol of the universe—might be incorporated into the temple's design to represent the interconnectedness of all existence and the divine presence at the center.

5) **Mythological Narratives:**
Ornate carvings and reliefs on temple walls often depict mythological stories from the religious tradition. These narratives serve as visual scriptures, conveying moral lessons, divine interactions, and the eternal struggle between good and evil. The temple becomes a living repository of sacred stories, allowing worshippers to engage with the mythology and gain insight into their faith.

6) **Pilgrimage Symbolism:**
Many temples are situated in remote or challenging locations, requiring pilgrims to embark on arduous journeys to reach them. This pilgrimage symbolism embodies the idea that the spiritual path is not easy; it requires dedication, sacrifice, and perseverance. The physical journey becomes a metaphor for the spiritual journey, symbolizing the devotee's quest for enlightenment.

7) **Offerings and Devotion:**
The design of temple spaces often includes areas for making offerings and expressing devotion. Altars, prayer halls, and incense burners serve as conduits for devotees to present their offerings and engage in acts of worship. These spaces symbolize the exchange between the human and divine realms, where offerings signify gratitude and surrender to the higher powers.

D) **Societal Symbolism:**
Beyond their religious and spiritual significance, temples often carry profound societal symbolism. These architectural marvels not only serve as places of worship but also reflect the values, social dynamics, and cultural aspirations of the societies that built them.

1) **Identity and Heritage:**
Temples are powerful symbols of cultural identity and heritage. The architectural style, artistic elements, and construction techniques used in temples reflect the unique characteristics of a particular civilization. Temples become tangible expressions of a society's artistic achievements, transmitting their cultural legacy to future generations.

2) **Social Order and Power:**
Throughout history, temples have been commissioned by rulers and elite classes, underscoring their authority and influence. The grandeur and scale of temple

architecture can serve as symbols of the power and prestige of ruling entities. Temple complexes may also include administrative and educational structures, reinforcing the role of religion in shaping societal order.

3) **Economic and Technological Advancements:**
The construction of monumental temples often requires significant resources, including manpower, materials, and engineering expertise. A society's ability to build and maintain such structures showcases its economic prosperity and technological prowess. Advanced architectural techniques, intricate carvings, and innovative engineering solutions demonstrate the level of sophistication achieved by a civilization.

4) **Cultural Syncretism:**
Many societies are characterized by cultural diversity and the merging of various traditions. Temples often embody this syncretism, incorporating architectural elements, artistic motifs, and rituals from multiple cultural sources. Such synthesis signifies the harmonious coexistence and blending of different cultural influences within a society.

5) **Communal Gathering and Identity:**
Temples serve as central gathering places for communities, hosting religious festivals, cultural events, and social gatherings. These events foster a sense of community identity and shared values. The temple complex becomes a focal point where people come together to celebrate, exchange ideas, and reinforce their social bonds.

6) **Moral and Ethical Values:**
The architectural design and decorative elements of temples often convey moral and ethical teachings. Sculptures, reliefs, and inscriptions depict virtues, ethical dilemmas, and mythological narratives that communicate societal values. By visually narrating these stories, temples serve as moral guides, shaping the ethical fabric of the society.

7) **Temporal Transcendence:**
The enduring nature of temple architecture transcends time, connecting the past, present, and future. Temples stand as symbols of continuity, reminding society of its roots and cultural legacy. They become touchstones through which individuals can reflect on the journey of their civilization across the ages.

3.4 Gandhara Style, Mathura Style, Naagar Style, Dravid Style:

The artistic landscape of India is adorned with diverse architectural styles, each a testament to the country's rich cultural tapestry. The Gandhara Style, originating in the crossroads of Central Asia, harmoniously fuses Greek, Roman, and Indian elements, with its intricate sculptures and cross-cultural symbolism. The Mathura Style, rooted in the northern heartland, emphasizes idealism and emotive expression, often portraying deities and figures with symbolic significance. Meanwhile, the Naagar Style, prevalent in the north, boasts towering shikharas and ornate carvings in its temple architecture, while the Dravid Style of the south is marked by majestic vimanas, elaborate gopurams, and intricate sculptures that encapsulate the spiritual essence of Hindu temple design. Together, these architectural styles weave an intricate narrative of India's artistic evolution, reflecting its historical, religious, and regional diversity.

3.4.1 Gandhara Style:

The Gandhara style of architecture, emerging from the heart of Central Asia, ventured into the diverse landscape of India, leaving an indelible imprint on the country's architectural tapestry. Rooted in the historical Gandhara region spanning parts of present-day Pakistan and Afghanistan, this architectural tradition bears witness to the rich cultural exchanges facilitated by the Silk Road. A fascinating amalgamation of Greek, Roman, Persian, and Indian influences, the Gandhara style encapsulates a harmonious confluence of aesthetics, spirituality, and craftsmanship.

1) **Historical and Geographical Context:**
   The Gandhara region, strategically situated along the Silk Road, emerged as a pivotal crossroads of civilizations. It played host to interactions between the Mauryan, Kushan, and Gupta empires, laying the foundation for the Gandhara style's evolution.

2) **Cultural Fusion and Synthesis:**
   The hallmark of Gandhara style architecture is its remarkable synthesis of diverse cultural influences. A medley of Hellenistic realism, Roman drapery, Persian motifs, and Indian spirituality converged to create a visual language that transcends conventional boundaries.

3) **Greek and Roman Aesthetics:**
   The interactions along the Silk Road deeply permeated Gandhara architecture. Greek and Roman aesthetics manifested through elements such as Corinthian and Ionic columns, pilasters, friezes, and the incorporation of realistic human forms.

4) **Sculptural Embellishments:**
   A defining feature of Gandhara style architecture is its intricate sculptural embellishments. Elaborate carvings, especially on facades, toranas, and narrative relief panels, often depicted Buddhist iconography, Jataka tales, and scenes from Buddha's life.

5) **Stupas and Chaityas:**
   The Gandhara style found its most profound expression in the construction of stupas, iconic Buddhist structures. These dome-shaped edifices, adorned with intricate carvings, narrated tales from the life of Buddha. The chaitya halls, sacred

spaces for congregational worship, showcased semi-circular apsidal plans and sculptural ornamentation.

6) **Greco-Roman Architectural Integration:**

Greco-Roman architectural elements seamlessly merged with the Gandhara style. Columns, pilasters, and intricate motifs like acanthus leaves and volutes were interwoven into stupas, monastic complexes, and temple facades.

7) **Buddhist Monastic Complexes:**

The Gandhara style's cross-cultural synthesis was especially evident in Buddhist monastic complexes. Viharas (monasteries) and stupas reflected architectural features influenced by diverse cultures, embodying the region's role as a melting pot of artistic ideas.

8) **Transmission of Buddhist Teachings:**

Gandhara sculptures and narrative relief panels served as visual conduits for Buddhist teachings. These artistic expressions facilitated the dissemination of Buddhist philosophy and narratives along the Silk Road.

9) **Aesthetic Continuation in Modern Times:**

Though the Gandhara style waned over time, its architectural elements have continued to influence contemporary architectural expressions. Modern structures incorporate Greco-Roman motifs and realistic sculptural techniques, testifying to the style's lasting legacy.

10) **Museums and Cultural Repositories:**

A multitude of Gandhara sculptures have found their way into museums and cultural institutions globally. These artifacts offer a glimpse into the artistic brilliance and cross-cultural interactions of antiquity.

11) **Source of Inspiration:**

The Gandhara style remains a wellspring of inspiration for artists, architects, and designers. Its harmonious fusion of cultural elements continues to serve as a muse for creating innovative expressions in the modern era.

12) **Legacy and Cultural Resonance:**

Gandhara style architecture, arising from the crossroads of Central Asia and embraced by the Indian subcontinent, epitomizes the interplay of cultures, religions, and artistic genius. Its confluence of Eastern and Western influences, its intricate sculptural embellishments, and its role in disseminating Buddhist teachings underscore its significance. The legacy of the Gandhara style resonates through time, reminding us of the enduring power of artistic expression to transcend temporal and geographical boundaries. It stands as a tribute to the remarkable ability of human creativity to forge connections across cultures and enrich our shared heritage.

3.4.2 Mathura Style:

The Mathura style of architecture, hailing from the northern heartland of India, encapsulates an artistic tradition characterized by idealized representations, emotive expression, and a profound connection to spiritual themes. Rooted in the historical city of Mathura, this architectural style emerged as a distinct expression of Indian art, deeply influenced by indigenous beliefs and religious practices.

1) **Historical and Cultural Context:**

   The city of Mathura, situated on the banks of the Yamuna River, holds significant religious and cultural importance in India. It was a thriving center for art, commerce, and spirituality, serving as a crucible for the evolution of the Mathura style.

2) **Emphasis on Idealism:**

   The Mathura style is marked by its emphasis on idealized representations. Sculptures, reliefs, and architectural elements often depict deities and figures in a manner that accentuates their spiritual significance rather than adhering strictly to naturalistic forms.

3) **Spiritual Expression:**

   Mathura style architecture excels in conveying spiritual and emotional depth through artistic expressions. Faces are adorned with serene expressions, and body postures communicate reverence, devotion, and a sense of transcendence.

4) **Narrative Detailing:**

   Carvings and reliefs in Mathura style architecture often tell stories from mythology and religious texts. These intricate depictions serve not only to illustrate narratives but also to evoke a sense of connection with the divine.

5) **Indigenous Aesthetic:**

   The Mathura style draws heavily from indigenous Indian aesthetic sensibilities, reflecting the region's cultural ethos. This connection to local traditions imbues the art with a distinct identity.

6) **Stone as Medium:**

   Mathura style architecture predominantly employed stone as its medium. The use of stone allowed for intricate detailing, durability, and a lasting legacy that has survived the passage of time.

7) **Temples and Sacred Structures:**

   The Mathura style's impact is particularly evident in temple architecture. These structures were designed not only as places of worship but also as living embodiments of the divine.

8) Iconography and Deities:

Mathura style architecture often centers on the depiction of deities, particularly those from Hindu mythology. The sculptures are characterized by graceful poses, elaborate headdresses, and intricate jewelry.

9) Religious and Symbolic Elements:

The architectural elements of Mathura style structures often carry deep religious and symbolic significance. Elements like pillars, brackets, and ornate facades communicate divine themes and spiritual narratives.

10) Legacy of Craftsmanship:

The Mathura style's legacy endures through its intricate craftsmanship, which continues to inspire artists and architects to this day. Its artistic sensibilities have influenced various Indian art forms and contemporary designs.

11) Preservation and Conservation:

While many original Mathura style structures have faced the challenges of time, efforts have been made to preserve and conserve the remaining artifacts, providing glimpses into the architectural brilliance of ancient Mathura.

12) Cultural Continuity:

The Mathura style architecture stands as a testament to India's rich artistic heritage and its seamless integration of spirituality with aesthetics. Its idealized representations, emotive expressions, and rootedness in indigenous culture continue to resonate through time, serving as a reminder of the profound relationship between art and spirituality. The Mathura style's enduring legacy is a testament to its ability to transcend epochs, making it an essential thread in the tapestry of Indian architectural history.

3.4.3 Naagar Style:

Naagar style architecture, also known as North Indian Temple Architecture, stands as a

Naagar style architecture, also known as North Indian Temple Architecture, stands as a grand testimony to the artistic brilliance of northern India. Rooted in the rich cultural and religious heritage of the region, this architectural style has left an indelible mark on the landscape, reflecting the spiritual devotion and cultural dynamism of the people.

1) Historical and Cultural Context:

The Naagar style originated in the northern regions of India, encompassing present-day states such as Uttar Pradesh, Rajasthan, and Madhya Pradesh. This style of architecture flourished during different historical periods, bearing witness to the socio-cultural transitions of the region.

2) Sacred Temples as Centerpieces:

At the heart of the Naagar style lays its association with temple architecture. These sacred structures served as vibrant centers of worship, education, and community engagement, embodying the spiritual essence of the people.

3) Shikhara: The Towering Symbol of Divinity:

One of the defining features of the Naagar style is the shikhara, a towering spire that crowns the sanctum of the temple. The shikhara's distinct design varies across regions, showcasing the diversity of North Indian temple architecture.

4) Curvilinear and Tiered Shikharas:

Naagar style shikharas often exhibit a curvilinear form, characterized by multiple tiers that gradually decrease in size as they ascend. These tiers are adorned with intricate carvings, reflecting the temple's spiritual narrative.

5) Ornate Facades and Mandapas:

The Naagar style places great emphasis on ornate facades and mandapas (pillared halls). These features are often adorned with intricate carvings, sculptures of deities, and depictions of mythological narratives.

6) Symbolism in Sculptural Embellishments:

Sculptural elements play a significant role in Naagar style architecture. Carvings often convey religious stories, philosophical concepts, and symbolic representations that resonate with devotees and visitors alike.

7) Inner Sanctum and Garbhagriha:

The inner sanctum, known as the garbhagriha, holds the main deity's shrine. It serves as the spiritual core of the temple, enveloping worshippers in an atmosphere of reverence and devotion.

8) Pillared Halls for Congregation:

Mandapas, or pillared halls, provide spaces for congregational gatherings, celebrations, and rituals. These halls facilitate communal engagement and foster a sense of togetherness.

9) Intricate Carvings and Ornamentation:

Naagar style architecture is renowned for its intricate carvings and ornamentation. The surfaces of temples are adorned with detailed motifs, floral patterns, divine figures, and scenes from epics.

10) Gopurams: Elaborate Entrance Gateways:

In some variations of the Naagar style, monumental entrance gateways, known as gopurams, are a prominent feature. These towering structures are intricately decorated with sculptures and serve as a gateway to the temple complex.

11) Cultural and Religious Continuity:

The Naagar style's enduring legacy is a testament to its seamless integration with the cultural and religious fabric of North India. Its architectural principles have influenced subsequent generations of architects and artists.

12) Legacy in Modern Times:

Naagar style architecture continues to inspire contemporary architects, artists, and designers. Its timeless elegance, profound symbolism, and spiritual resonance remind us of the enduring power of architecture to transcend time and connect people with the divine.

3.4.4 Dravid Style:

Dravid style architecture, a hallmark of South Indian temple design, stands as a testament to the rich cultural and religious heritage of the region. Rooted in spirituality and influenced by indigenous traditions, this architectural style has left an indelible mark on the landscape, reflecting the profound connection between art, devotion, and the divine.

1) **Historical and Cultural Context:**

   The Dravid style of architecture flourished in the southern regions of India, encompassing states like Tamil Nadu, Karnataka, and Andhra Pradesh. It emerged during different historical epochs, bearing witness to the diverse cultural tapestry of the region.

2) **Temples as Spiritual Sanctuaries:**

   At the heart of the Dravid style lays its association with temple architecture. Temples are not just places of worship; they are revered as divine abodes that foster a profound spiritual connection between devotees and the deities.

3) **Vimana: The Towering Sanctum:**

   A defining feature of Dravid style architecture is the vimana, the towering and intricately adorned tower that shelters the main deity's shrine (garbhagriha). The vimana is a visual manifestation of the spiritual journey towards divinity.

4) **Pyramidal Vimanas with Tiered Roofs:**

   Dravid style vimanas often assume a pyramidal form, with multiple tiered roofs that gradually decrease in size as they ascend. Each tier is adorned with sculptures, carvings, and intricate ornamentation.

5) **Intricate Carvings and Sculptures:**

   Dravid style architecture places great emphasis on intricate carvings and sculptures. These artistic elements depict deities, mythological narratives, celestial beings, and divine symbols, enhancing the spiritual ambiance of the temple.

6) Gopurams: Towering Entrance Gateways:

A distinctive feature of Dravid style temples is the towering entrance gateway, known as the gopuram. These gateways are adorned with elaborate sculptures and serve as a symbolic threshold between the worldly realm and the sacred space.

7) Courtyards and Pillared Halls:

Dravid style temples often feature spacious courtyards and pillared halls that serve as congregational spaces for rituals, festivals, and gatherings. These areas foster a sense of community and devotion.

8) Symbolism in Architecture:

Architectural elements in Dravid style structures are replete with symbolism. Pillars, brackets, and carvings convey intricate philosophical concepts, mythological stories, and religious motifs.

9) Inner Sanctum and Garbhagriha:

The inner sanctum, known as the garbhagriha, houses the main deity's shrine. It is the spiritual nucleus of the temple, enveloping devotees in an atmosphere of reverence and devotion.

10) Continued Relevance and Devotion:

Dravid style architecture remains integral to the cultural and religious fabric of South India. Devotees continue to engage with these temples as sacred spaces for worship, festivals, and spiritual contemplation.

11) Influence on Contemporary Design:

The Dravid style's timeless elegance and spiritual resonance continue to inspire modern architects, artists, and designers. Its influence can be seen in various architectural expressions that draw from its aesthetic principles.

12) A Living Legacy:

Dravid style architecture stands as a living testament to the artistic brilliance, cultural continuity, and profound spirituality of South India. Its intricate detailing, sacred narratives, and architectural symbolism remind us of the enduring power of architecture to connect humanity with the divine.

♦♦♦

Review Questions

Q.1. Answer the Following Questions:

1) Explain in detail about the Bhinbetka Architecture in India.
2) Discuss about the Bagh Caves.
3) Explain in detail about the Ajanta Caves.
4) Write about the Ellora Caves.
5) Discuss in detail about the Tanjore Caves.
6) Explain in detail about Religious Symbolism of Temple Architecture.
7) Discuss about the Societal Symbolism of Temple Architecture.
8) Explain in detail Gandhar Style Architecture.
9) Discuss about the Mathura Style.
10) Explain in detail Naagar Style.
11) Write about the Dravid Style.

Q.3. Write Short Notes on:

1) Bhimbetka.
2) Bagh Caves.
3) Ajanta Caves.
4) Ellora Caves.
5) Tanjore Caves.
6) Gandhar Style.
7) Mathura Style.
8) Naagar Style.
9) Dravid Style.

♦♦♦